WORK AND WELFARE IN BRITAIN AND THE USA

By the same author

ON RELIEF : THE ECONOMICS OF POVERTY AND PUBLIC WELFARE

INCENTIVES AND PLANNING IN SOCIAL POLICY : ESSAYS IN
HEALTH, EDUCATION AND WELFARE *(co-editor with S. M. Miller)*

WORK AND WELFARE IN BRITAIN AND THE USA

Bruno Stein

A HALSTED PRESS BOOK

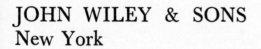

JOHN WILEY & SONS
New York

First published 1976 by
THE MACMILLAN PRESS LTD
London and Basingstoke

Published in the U.S.A.
by Halsted Press, a Division of
John Wiley & Sons, Inc., New York

Printed in Great Britain

Library of Congress Cataloging in Publication Data

Stein, Bruno, 1930–
  Work and welfare in Britain and the U.S.

  Bibliography : p.
  1. Manpower policy—Great Britain. 2. Economic security—
Great Britain. 3. Public welfare—United States. 4. Public
welfare—Great Britain. 5. Manpower Policy—United States. I.
Title.

HD5767.S72   362.5'0941   75–44186
ISBN 0–470–15007–6

To my teacher, colleague, and friend
Lois MacDonald, Ph.D.
Professor Emeritus of Economics
New York University
this work is dedicated with respect, affection, and hope of approval.

Contents

List of Tables

List of Figures

Preface

Social policies that have a high emotional content do not easily lend themselves to rational analysis. Income maintenance policies have this characteristic, and properly so. They deal with the lives and well-being of working people and of poor people. The generosity of the policies – their relative benefit levels, extent of coverage, and method of financing – are tests of a society's standard of social decency and of its sense of distributive justice. The distributions of income and wealth are, after all, the stuff of which wars and revolutions are made. Poverty induces pain and rage in its victims, and invites feelings of compassion and fear from among the community's affluents. None of these emotions is conducive to cool-headed analysis and to the formulation of rational policy.

None the less, if we wish to solve complex social problems, or substantially ameliorate them, then a rational analytic attitude is a necessity. This involves specifying the objectives of a social policy and designing it so that the desired outcome is a predictable consequence of the policy, given the available state of knowledge. It may well be true that large parliamentary democracies are not capable of rational social planning and must always rely on muddling through. I sincerely hope that this is not the case.

The analytical approach taken in this book is politically neutral. It is intended to be applicable to western industrial societies irrespective of their forms of social organization, as long as they rely on labor markets as the primary tool for the allocation of human resources and the distribution of income. It is, therefore, not my purpose to give aid and comfort to liberals and socialists, nor to conservatives of either the *laissez-faire* or the statist varieties. Judging from the reactions of those who have read preliminary drafts of this book, I am likely to offend people in all political camps. My purpose, however, is to contribute to the technology of social problem-solving, and I leave ideological matters to those who prefer that sort of thing. As an American I do not, of course, have a licence to criticize British social policy. I find that writing about another nation's policy issues is a good way to gain perspective on one's own, and I have learned a good deal about my own country from this exercise. I hope that British readers, in reading a foreigner's view of their system, will also gain some insights therefrom, as well as from the presentation of the American policies that is given in this book.

1975 may be a poor year in which to base a microeconomic policy analysis on the assumption that macroeconomic policy can sustain full employment as a more or less normal state of affairs. Only a few years ago, much was made of the emergence of a new post-industrial society from which scarcity was to be banished. In this brave new world it was hoped by some – and feared by others – that leisure would be in excess supply. The hard times of the 1970s remind us that an excess supply of leisure can also be found in the form of unemployment, and that a persistently high level of unemployment is a policy problem of acute importance. The failure of simple Keynsian policy in Europe and the USA is forcing economists and policy-makers to take a closer look at the structural problems that have commonly been omitted from consideration in the conventional Keynsian (or even monetarist) models. Perhaps the work contained herein can contribute, in a small way, toward improvements in the theory of employment by stressing the need to examine the malfunctioning of labor markets in greater institutional detail than has heretofore been fashionable.

The American parts of this book reflect my long standing research interest in the economics of public assistance. The British parts are based on a research project I conducted in Britain in 1972–3. The initial findings from that project were reported to the Manpower Administration of the US Department of Labor, which has non-exclusive rights to that report. The present volume has considerably expanded on the initial report, information has been updated, and some of the more egregious errors have been removed. Unless otherwise indicated, benefit levels are for 1974.

A study of this sort must rely on impressions as well as on data. I was fortunate in receiving considerable help from British sources. This included visits to the sites of centers operated by the Department of Employment and the Department of Health and Social Security, and interviews with civil servants both at operating and at higher levels. In many cases, their comments were quite frank (and off the record). My thanks go to all of them, and to the two departments for the official and courteous cooperation that was extended to me. DHSS made some unpublished data available to me, as did Messrs Adrian Ziderman of Queen Mary College and Michael Hill of the University of Oxford, and I want to express my gratitude for their kindness.

Additional thanks are due to the staff of the Department of Social

Science and Administration at the London School of Economics who invited me to be an Academic Visitor, and who gave of their time to teach me the ropes and to establish contacts for me. Professors Garth Plowman and Brian Abel-Smith were especially helpful, as was Mr David Piachaud, and I benefited greatly from the advice of the late Professor Richard Titmuss. My research headquarters were established at the Centre for Studies in Social Policy, which honored me with a Visiting Fellowship. I am especially indebted to A. R. Isserlis, Rudolf Klein, Vera Morris, the invaluable Susan Johnson, and my fellow visiting fellow, Professor Shlakman of Columbia University. Sir John Walley was kind enough to comment on an early draft of the manuscript.

On this side of the pond, I want to acknowledge the very helpful assistance and criticism of Miles L. Wortman. My wife, Judith A. Stein, receives my thanks not only for her trenchant editorial comments, but also for her willingness to spend a year with me in foreign climes : it could have been a disaster. I am grateful to the Manpower Administration and to its Director of Research and Development, Howard Rosen, for the grant that enabled me to visit Britain. Additional financial help came from the Arts and Science Research Fund and the Institute of Labor Relations of New York University. None of the foregoing persons and institutions are responsible for the errors that have undoubtedly found their way into the book. Needless to say, the work does not represent the opinion or policy of anyone except the author.

List of Abbreviations

ADC	Aid to Dependent Children (US)
AFDC	Aid to Families with Dependent Children (US)
AFDC–UP	Aid to Families with Dependent Children–Unemployed Parent (US)
CETA	Comprehensive Employment and Training Act (US)
CPAG	Child Poverty Action Group (UK)
DE	Department of Employment (UK)
DHSS	Department of Health and Social Security (UK)
ESA	Employment Services Agency (UK)
FAM	Family Allowances (UK)
FAP	Family Assistance Plan (US)
FERA	Federal Emergency Relief Administration (US)
FIS	Family Income Supplement (UK)
GA	General Assistance (US)
GTCs	Government Training Centres (UK)
HMSO	Her Majesty's Stationery Office (UK)
IRUs	Industrial Rehabilitation Units (UK)
ITBs	Industrial Training Boards (UK)
JOBS	Job Opportunities in the Business Sector (US)
MDTA	Manpower Development and Training Act (US)
Medicaid	Medical Assistance (US)
Medicare	Medical Insurance for the Aged (US)
NA	National Assistance (UK)
NI	National Insurance (UK)
NYC	Neighborhood Youth Corps (US)
OASDHI	Old Age, Survivors' Disability and Health Insurance (US)
OECD	Organization for Economic Cooperation and Development (International)
RB	Redundancy Benefit (UK)
SB	Supplementary Benefit (UK)
TOPS	Training Opportunities Scheme (UK)

TSA   Training Services Agency (UK)
UB   Unemployment Benefit (UK)
UI   Unemployment Insurance (US)
WIN   Work Incentive Program (US)

1 Work, Welfare and Training

INTRODUCTION
This study explores the relationship between manpower policy and income maintenance by examining the British experience against the parallel American policies. Such comparison is possible for several reasons: both countries have some similarity in their legal and cultural heritage, including a common origin in the Poor Law for their public assistance programs; relatively high rates of unemployment even in boom times, as compared to other industrial nations; ethnic and racial problems that carry over into labor markets; and a degree of under-investment in human capital, especially among persons now in their middle years. There are differences, to be sure. Americans do not think of themselves as having a welfare state, although they are moving toward one by the accretion of their programs. By comparison, Britain has an advanced welfare state, although it ranks well below western Europe in the per cent of GNP at factor cost that is devoted to social security spending.[1]

The intent of this work is to contribute to the emerging literature on work and welfare, as well as to the exploration of comparative social policy. Scholars like Wilensky are seeking the broad structural and cultural determinants of the welfare state in an effort to understand the varying allocations of scarce resources in the social policy programs of industrial nations.[2] Others, like Kaim-Caudle, have given us detailed comparative analyses of specific policies that apply to unemployment, disability, old age and family endowment.[3] The approach of this work lies somewhere in between.

My concern is with the construction of policies that are workable – that do what they are supposed to do. Welfare policies, for example, have often failed to achieve their sponsors' aims. My emphasis, therefore, is on the pragmatic. Given the broader determinants of a nation's social security and other social policies, and given the details of various programs within these policies, how can policies be shaped so as to accomplish their goals? Social policy is rarely developed as a complete and rational package, and I have tried to resist the academic temptation to infer that there must be considered policies and good respectable reasons behind each legislative act. In practice, social legislation is born of conflicting goals and interests, and its various parts grow by accretion. The process compounds existing goal conflicts within the system. As changes in social goals and social problems proceed, new policies are added, existing policies develop clienteles with vested interests, and the resultant policy set can behave irrationally with respect to any or all goals.

The academic temptation to which I succumb is to analyse policy from the viewpoint of the economist. This sees a community in which resources are scarce, and in which people's economic behavior is influenced by their self-interest as they perceive it. People try to obtain scarce resources as best they can, using the means at their command : their wit, their skills, their wealth, and their access to power. The competition takes place in a framework of custom and law in which individuals may forego the pursuit of anti-social goals, perhaps because of their social conscience or their fear of reprisal. The economic view leads one to believe that policies that persistently ask people to behave irrationally with respect to their daily bread and butter are likely to encounter considerable difficulties in their operation.

In practice, it is not unusual to encounter such policy situations. Two social policies may co-exist, one which asks people to behave in Mode *A*, and another which provides an incentive to behave in Mode *B*. Each policy, taken by itself, may have been sensible at its inception, and have been directed at separate constituencies. Now, the economy has changed, the constituencies overlap, and the policies interact. At the margin, some people who are asked to behave in Mode *A* will, instead, respond to the incentives of Mode *B*. When enough people behave this way, a policy problem can be said to exist. Resources flow in directions that are contrary to the expressed wishes of the policy. The 'poor unfortunate recipients of the taxpayers gracious bounty' (in the United States), or in the 'rightful claimants of temporary supplements' (in the United Kingdom) become, in a crisis, a bunch of chiselers or scroungers. In fact they are neither wicked nor depraved, but are people who are making the best of a bad situation by behaving sensibly instead of stupidly.

The central thesis of this study is that income maintenance policies and manpower policies are not, and cannot be, independent of each other. Both address themselves to the labor market behavior of individuals and families. Both must be viewed as policy systems that are composed of subsystems. The subsystems can interact in two ways : (1) when they are additive, and (2) when the presence of one affects behavior with respect to the other. The systems, in turn, also interact. The interactions may be functional or dysfunctional with respect to their given policy goals or sets of goals. All this can be observed in the United States and Great Britain.

Put another way, the goals of the policies may be in consonance or conflict, and the same is true of the means that are intended to achieve these goals. Conflicting means or goals will inhibit the functioning of a policy. Consonant goals and means will facilitate the functioning of a policy, although they will not guarantee its success.

It is never possible to develop public policy that is completely successful with reference to its stated goals. It is possible, however, to facilitate success by minimizing those policy aspects that are likely to lead to failure, and enhancing those that are likely to bring success. Of course, this requires policy-makers to define their goals and to specify their criteria of success. The democratic political process, on the other hand, involves a certain amount of concealment of this information in order to achieve a necessary degree of consensus. In an imperfect world, it may not be possible to construct perfectly rational social policies. Nevertheless, it may be worth while to try.

Backgrounds

The Poor Law of 1601 serves as the traditional starting point for relief in both Great Britain and the United States. A relationship between income maintenance for able-bodied persons and their labor market behavior has been recognized since even before this legislation. At times, the concern has been a political obsession. During the debates over the British Poor Law Reform of 1834, it was feared that the guaranteed income of the Speenhamland relief system would demoralize the British yeomanry and turn eager workers into layabouts.[4] The American tradition, which was influenced by the British debates, was to establish relief categories which generally excluded those persons who could be expected to work for a living. The requirement that these 'work-eligible' people who received assistance actively look for work as an alternative to relief became common to both countries, except that the British now exclude unsupported mothers whereas the Americans include them. The basic principle is the same in both countries. The differences are in the specific application of the rule.

The idea that able-bodied persons in need of relief might benefit from training is also an old one, but governments did not until more recent times view the training of adults as a public function (the workhouse was not a training school, to put it mildly). During the 1862 cotton famine in Britain, training schools in Lancashire taught sewing to girls, and men and boys were exposed to 'book-learning' in an effort to enhance their employability. It is noteworthy that these activities were regarded as 'test work', i.e. a condition for obtaining relief.[5] The 1911 Unemployment Insurance Act in Britain empowered insurance officers to compel applicants to take courses in technical instruction where this was likely to diminish the Fund's outlays in the longer run. More formal training provisions for unemployed men developed in Britain in the 1920s, first for younger men, and then for middle aged men up to forty-five years of age.[6]

The role of government in providing employment services dates back to the institution of unemployment benefits on a social insurance basis. Government as a provider of training to adults is essentially a post-World War II concept. European governments led the way with the development of manpower policies to relocate and retrain workers. The primary motive behind the European programs was economic rather than social. The intent of such measures was to relieve shortages of skilled labor, increase productivity, and facilitate economic growth. Social goals were secondary. In Britain, the manpower policies that emerged in the early 1960s were intended to help the economy move out of its stop–go trap and into a sustained phase of economic growth.

The Americans, on the other hand, approached manpower policy with a more mixed set of goals. One important aim was the reduction of structural unemployment. A second one was a social goal : enabling people to earn a proper income on the labor market.

The initial Manpower Development and Training Act emerged in the United States in 1962 as a political response to relatively high levels of unemployment and the belief that widespread job vacancies existed.[7] The Act was the first substantial attempt by the American government to provide training for able-bodied adults. Congressmen who voted for the Act were also aware of a secondary role to be played by training programs : income maintenance for unemployed workers who would receive training allowances. The initial targets were unemployed but otherwise employable workers who had a high likelihood of success in completing the courses of training and finding available work.

In the following years, however, emphasis began to shift to the socially disadvantaged and harder to employ. Maldistribution of income became an important policy concern. These were the years of the War on Poverty when Americans hoped to use social policy to end poverty in their country. Many of the policies were manpower programs to aid potentially employable poor people, especially youth. By 1966 the overall rate of unemployment had fallen low enough (under the stimulus of the Vietnam war) to make inflation more worrisome than unemployment. Unemployment was so low that workers in the mainstream had no difficulty in getting jobs. Accordingly, the training emphasis shifted even further toward providing skills for the disadvantaged. In 1967 Congress required adult recipients of Aid to Families with Dependent Children (AFDC), most of whom were unsupported mothers, to register for work or training as a condition of receiving aid. A number of states followed suit with their General Assistance programs for persons who did not qualify for AFDC. For example, in New York, the policy of requiring work from recipients is known as Workfare. Thus, American manpower policy received another goal : to reduce the level of welfare expenditures.[8]

The Macroeconomic Context

As shown above, there are two policy systems that pertain to potentially employable but unemployed persons. One is income support, where work-eligible individuals are expected to achieve employed status as quickly as possible. The second is manpower policy – especially training schemes – which can enable persons who lack salable skills to acquire them. The linkage – or lack of linkage – between manpower policy and income support is a major topic of this book.

It must be stressed that both of the policy systems will have different behaviors and different functions according to whether overall levels of unemployment are high or low. High unemployment places burdens on income support systems, and removes some of the rationale for manpower policies. When there are few jobs available on the completion of the course, the question arises : training for what? In the absence of employment opportunities, training schemes with allowances may serve the very useful function of being disguised forms of income maintenance. In addition, they may redistribute income among workers by redistributing access to skills and jobs. Finally, an increased labor supply in particular occupations might reduce relative wages in these occupations; given the elasticity of labor demand in these markets, the lower wages might, marginally, increase employment. Presumably, the unionized sector of the labor market would be insulated from this effect, and the unionized sector is likely to have the higher paying jobs.

Persistently high unemployment in the economy generates a population this is persistently out of the labor market. Unemployment is not evenly or randomly distributed. Workers with good jobs hang on to them. Turnover and attrition do provide some opportunities to the unemployed, even during severe recessions. However, the opportunities favor workers who do not have an extensive history of unemployment, such as young workers who are new entrants into the labor market and experienced workers with relatively shorter spells of unemployment. When this is the case, income maintenance policies are more than temporary supplements to the unemployed. They are also needed to support a more or less permanent class of idle poor.

On the other hand, low unemployment raises both the economic and social payoffs to manpower policies, and emphasizes the short-run functions of income maintenance. It is in good times that individual choices between work and welfare payments become an issue, and questions of work incentives become more than academic. For this reason, the analysis contained in this work is most relevant to a more or less full employment economy. The distribution of unemployment in a depressed economy is a subject for political rather than economic analysis and lies beyond the scope of this book.

The Plan of the Work

This work arises from a one-year study of British welfare and manpower policies conducted by the author in 1972–3. The results of that study are the focal point of the book, and serve to provide a theoretical structure for the analysis of welfare systems. The problems at issue are first placed in a comparative setting in Chapter 2, which gives an overview and some analysis of American income support schemes and the principal manpower training policies. The British experience is developed in the three chapters that follow : the first, Chapter 3, provides a background to British social security; Chapter 4 examines income support programs in some detail to isolate the interrelationships of their component parts. Reference is also made to the phenomenon of the poverty trap. Chapter 5 looks at the control procedures used in Britain to ration access to the public assistance system. Manpower training policies and their relevance to income support are covered in Chapter 6. In the final chapter conclusions are drawn which, it is hoped, are relevant to the development of rational policy.

Two notes of caution are in order : (1) Any international comparison is likely to encounter difficulties arising from cultural differences, and the similarity between the English and American languages does not always prevent misunderstandings. (2) Cultural backgrounds and value judgments have a way of distorting an analytic signal. I have, as always, sought to play the role of the value-free analyst, in the scientific traditions of economics. This may make the work seem rather more cold-blooded than I really intended it to be. In fair warning to the reader, my utopia is a society with rather less inequality of income and wealth, and rather more equality of opportunity than are currently found in Britain or the United States. It is a place in which every person is at minimum entitled to as good a job as he is capable of learning to do.

2 Income Support and Manpower Programs in the USA

Social insurance came later to the United States than to almost all other industrial nations. The earliest social insurance provisions were Workmen's Compensation programs for industrial injuries. These date back to the first decade of the twentieth century, and it is noteworthy that they were really compulsory private insurance required of employers. Growing in an unplanned fashion, Workmen's Compensation programs owe their development to legislative and judicial actions in several states that facilitated damage suits by injured workers, thus necessitating insurance on the part of employers. In order to make such insurance less costly, the Workmen's Compensation laws were enacted. In return for eliminating the issue of negligence – was the worker careless or the employer negligent – they removed the right of injured workers to sue for damages and substituted a scale of allowance plus medical costs. The insurance is genuine, in the sense that an actuarial basis exists for it, and virtually all of it is written by private companies. Where state-owned companies exist, they do so largely for the purpose of covering poor risks. All other form of social insurance, with minor exception of state experimentation, awaited the passage of the Social Security Act of 1935.

The Social Security Act imported the long-standing European concepts of social insurance, including the levying of earmarked payroll taxes payable into special funds, and the 'right' to benefits as having been earned by previous taxable participation in the labor market. The Act initially created a federally administered program of old age pensions, formally known as Old Age Insurance (OAI) and popularly called Social Security. Survivors' Insurance (SI) was added in 1940 to provide benefits for the widows of workers who were caring for minor children. Benefits in both programs were earnings-related between a minimum and a maximum and varied by family size. They were set too low to enable the claimant to enjoy a living standard anywhere near the previous earnings, except in a minor way. The purposes of the earnings limitation were (1) to get claimants out of the labor market in a period of job scarcity, (2) to encourage thrift during the productive life of the wage-earner, and (3) to encourage the flow of income transfers within the extended family and thus minimize the role of the government as the provider of benefits. Public assistance, however, could be used to supplement social insurance benefits up to the standard of need set by each state.[1]

The Social Security system was further extended in 1956 by the addition of Disability Insurance (DI) for permanently disabled workers and their dependents. Medical insurance for the aged (HI) was added in 1966. Thus, OASDHI (i.e. the combined OAI, SI, DI and HI programs) constitutes the federal government's social insurance system for the broad mass of American workers.

The original 1935 Act also created a system of Unemployment Insurance (UI), comparable in many respects to the present British unemployment benefit system of National Insurance. Unlike OASDHI, Unemployment Insurance was not made uniform across the country. Congress legislated the minimum standards for the system, but left it to the states to administer and to finance through a payroll tax on employers. The proceeds of the tax are deposited in each state's account in a federal trust fund. This means that standards of eligibility and benefit levels vary considerably from state to state and reflect both the local economies and social decisions regarding benefit levels and wages. All benefits are earnings related, subject to a maximum. As a general principle, benefits are supposed to be about 50 per cent of wages. Since maximum benefits have risen more slowly than money wages, the result is that, on average, benefits equal about one-third of the wage. However, eleven states provide additional allowances for dependents.[2]

The usual maximum duration of unemployment benefits is twenty-six weeks. In recent years, a number of states have entered into a federal program that provides for extended benefits of an additional thirteen weeks when unemployment reaches certain levels. Payment for such extensions come from funds in addition to those deposited in the trust fund, thus breaching the principle of 'sound' financing. Temporary 'emergency' provisions were made in 1974 and 1975 to extend benefit duration to a maximum of sixty-five weeks. One of the arguments in favor of the extension was that it keeps people off welfare rolls, presumably sparing them the stigma of public charity associated with public assistance and relieving the states of the costs of this income support.

The orginal Social Security Act kept coverage in OASDHI fairly narrow by omitting such categories as agricultural workers, employees of very small enterprises, the non-profit sector, and the public sector. Over the years, coverage in OASDHI has broadened considerably. Each extension 'blanketed in' workers who paid very little in taxes and received full pension benefits. At present, about 90 per cent of workers are in covered employment. The states have similarly broadened their UI coverage somewhat, and about 80 per cent of the labor force works in jobs covered by unemployment benefits. Collectively bargained unemployment benefits to supplement UI exist in a number of industries like auto and steel. Here, it should be noted, the 'insurance' is real in that the enterprises' liabilities are limited to the size of the fund and benefits cease when the fund is exhausted.

THE DEVELOPMENT OF PUBLIC ASSISTANCE

Public assistance dates back to the first British settlers who brought with them the English Poor Law. As I have noted elsewhere,[3] the English Poor Law traditions were characterized by (1) repression, (2) local financing and administration, (3) economizing, i.e. minimizing costs by achieving the economies of scale available in the poorhouse, (4) a work ethic, (5) a social distinction between the 'deserving' and the 'undeserving' poor, and (6) the stigma attached to asking for charity or 'going on the county'. At the beginning of the twentieth century, public assistance measures were essentially carried out by local governments, with some coordination and subvention from state Boards of Charity. There was no uniform system in the form of a national law, and most states did not even have uniform provisions within their borders.

The foundations for a national public assistance system were laid during the Great Depression. The severe economic setback that began in the United States in 1929 necessitated great outlays for the relief of unemployment as well as for the relief of other poverty. Before the advent of the New Deal administration of Franklin D. Roosevelt in 1933, such relief was believed to be the responsibility – if at all – of states and localities, and of private charity. However, the very economic forces that generated the need for relief reduced the ability of the states and localities to finance such relief. Tax revenues fell sharply after 1929, together with the borrowing power of sub-federal units of government. In the private sector, declining profits and capital losses sharply curtailed the flow of funds to private charity. A number of states, notably including New York, formed statewide relief systems in order to rationalize the availability and flow of relief funds throughout their jurisdictions. Roosevelt, who was Governor of New York from 1928 to 1932, brought his state's experience to Washington when he became President. One of the first New Deal measures enacted at the request of the new administration was the Federal Emergency Relief Administration (FERA), which disbursed federal money to State Emergency Relief Administrations created for the purpose of providing a dole to the unemployed.

FERA was intended to be a stopgap measure, and was supplanted by work-relief programs such as the Works Progress Administration (WPA) and the Civilian Conservation Corps (CCC). However, the federal government soon found itself under political pressure to enact social insurance measures, especially old age pensions, and to make some provision for the relief of other poverty. Roosevelt wanted to minimize the long-term role of the federal government as a relief agency. The resulting Social Security Act of 1935, which had both social insurance and public assistance parts, reflects the traditional and constitutional perceptions of the time as to the proper roles of federal and state governments in this type of endeavor.

The planners of the Social Security Act saw a relatively narrow scope for the federal government's role in public assistance. The foremost need was for Old Age Assistance (OAA, the public assistance version of Old Age Insurance OAI). The problem was that OAI would not begin to pay benefits until five years after the enactment of the law. This would mean that a substantial number of persons would reach retirement age in the interim, and for a generation thereafter, who had little or no coverage. To deal with this, the Act created a set of minimum standards for OAA programs to be administered by states, with the costs to be shared between the states and the federal government. States could, if they chose, redelegate administration of the program to their localities, and eleven states did this on a cost-sharing basis. Since all states now had emergency relief agencies, these were transformed into state welfare departments.

Successful lobbying by private charitable agencies for the blind led to the inclusion of a similar provision, called Aid to the Blind (AB) in the Act. An amendment in 1950 added Aid to the Permanently and Totally Disabled (APTD). Together with OAA, these were known as the adult categories. In 1974, the adult categories were federalized into one means tested pension system entitled Supplemental Security Income (SSI).

Another group for whom some political sympathy existed, and where there was a great need, were fatherless children. Aid to Dependent Children (ADC, later renamed Aid to Families with Dependent Children, AFDC) was added in the original bill, with a benefit structure lower than that for the other categories. The children were viewed as belonging to the 'deserving poor' – orphans and children raised by widows. However, the 1940 amendments that created Survivors' Insurance altered the political potency of this constituency by removing from the ADC clientele the more 'deserving' group : the children and widows of workers who had coverage under social insurance and thus had a record of attachment to the labor force. War veterans and their widows, also a 'deserving' group, had (and still have) special programs funded separately by the federal government's Veterans' Administration. This left, in the remaining pool of potential eligibles, the unsupported mothers of illegitimate children, and deserted mothers. Given the nature of American labor markets and the position of blacks on the income distribution, it is not astonishing that blacks were overrepresented among the claimants in this category. Although the program was not politically popular, its low take-up kept it out of the public eye until the 1960s, when the number of claimants began to soar.

In the 1960s, public assistance programs came to be known as 'welfare', because they were administered by agencies generally called Welfare Departments. With the removal of the former adult categories into the SSI program, the term 'welfare' now principally denotes Aid to Families with Dependent Children. Unsupported mothers who are claimants are known colloquially as 'welfare mothers'. Persons who receive public assistance are said to be 'on relief' or 'on welfare'.

I have omitted from consideration a large number of lesser benefit programs, such as free school breakfasts and lunches for needy children, public housing, rent subsidies, and supplemental feeding for pregnant and lactating women.[4] However two additional programs must be mentioned here : Medical Assistance, commonly called Medicaid, and the Food Stamp program.

The 1966 reform that enacted medical insurance for the aged (Medicare) provided a parallel provision for the poor (old and young) in the public assistance system. Medicaid covers all medical and hospital fees, including pharmaceuticals. This makes it the only program with complete coverage available in the United States, since both private insurance and Medicare have limits beyond which payment ceases. Medicaid is available to all AFDC recipients. Twenty-four states also offer it to the medically indigent, i.e. persons whose means are sufficient, except for their health care costs, to keep them off welfare.

The absence of comprehensive national health insurance or of a national health service puts a heavier burden on income maintenance in the United States than in Great Britain. To some extent, this is merely an accounting difference : medical resources devoted to the poor are not a separate item in the British accounts, whereas they appear – very visibly – as an item in the American public assistance data.

As of 1974, the Food Stamp program had developed into a minimum income guarantee. It was serving thirteen million Americans, of whom about ten million were also receiving welfare payments. The basic guarantee for a family of four with no income is $1704 per year. The benefit loss rate with respect to income is about 30 per cent, which means that the program can serve as a low wage supplement with a negative tax feature. The food stamp bonus – the difference between the cost of the stamps and their par value – is not counted as income for tax or welfare purposes. Accordingly, families that are entirely dependent on welfare pay nothing for the stamps and receive the entire bonus. This has resulted in a substantial improvement in the income of the welfare poor, especially in the low benefit states of the South where the addition of food stamps literally doubled family income.

SOCIAL INSURANCE VERSUS PUBLIC ASSISTANCE

The foregoing pages show that American income maintenance schemes developed into those that are primarily social insurance and those that are primarily public (or social) assistance. Although this dichotomy is not a precise one, the classification conveys a certain amount of information about the origin of programs, their administration, scope of coverage, and public attitudes.

Social insurance comprises a cluster of programs to 'insure' against the contingency that a family may suffer from a cessation of earned income that stems from the death, disability, unemployment, or retirement of a breadwinner. In the United States, at least, the relevant contingency pertains to labor market income, and the system hinges on the attachment by the individual, or household head, to the labor market. Indeed, attachment must be successful in the form of employment covered by the system, since participation is possible only when earmarked payroll taxes are paid into a fund that finances the benefits. Payment of these taxes through the employment process means that potential benefits are 'earned' and assume the character of a property right. Accordingly, they are not subject to a means test, although they may be subject to a test of currently earned income. The logic of the earned income test is that loss of earnings is the insurable contingency in question.

Public assistance, on the other hand, partakes of the character of public charity, with its attendant stigmas. There is no pretense that benefits were 'earned' by previous payment of taxes, nor is there even an attenuated link between past earnings, if any, and benefits. Payment is made out of revenues collected by taxing the general public. Benefit levels are estimates of a sort of social minimum for a family that has no other means of support. Hence, a means test is generally encountered in public assistance.

The criteria that distinguish between social insurance and public assistance in the United States can be spelled out in some further detail. As noted above, the relevant contingency is the loss of labor market income by the individual or head of household. Coverage in the social insurance system comes from having worked for a minimum specified period of time in a job, and having had taxes paid into the proper government fund. The presence of the funds symbolizes the insurance aspect of the programs, although, as a practical matter, the funds are bookkeeping devices rather than actual financial reserves. Thus, the Social Security Trust Fund, which deals with Old Age, Survivors Disability and Health Insurance, is credited with the payroll taxes collected from workers and employers. The monies themselves, however, are mingled with other revenues collected by the US Treasury, and the Fund receives, instead, interest-bearing obligations of the United States that are directly issued by the Treasury. State payroll taxies levied to support the unemployment insurance system are similarly deposited in a federally administered trust fund in which each state has an account. A state that is overdrawn may borrow from the federal government, but the possibility that a state may have to curtail benefits because its account is exhausted is politically remote – indeed, probably impossible.

The symbolic aspect of insurance is reflected also in the pseudo-actuarial notions that are used. It is, of course, simply impossible to make actuarial estimates of unemployment in an unplanned economy. The best one can do is estimate the incidence of unemployment claims under various levels of aggregate unemployment and hope that the macroeconomic policy-makers will be able to maintain the level of unemployment within reasonable, i.e. politically acceptable, bounds. It is a hope that is often disappointed.

Another departure from actuarial principles is found in the level of benefits. This is commonly based on current estimates of social adequacy rather than the value of previous contributions. Although an increase in current benefit levels may be accompanied by an increase in the applicable tax rates, an intertemporal transfer is clearly involved. In the case of Old Age Insurance, where benefits have been adjusted upward over time and are now indexed to the Consumer Price Index, the transfer of income is intergenerational. Taxes are paid by currently employed workers and the benefits from these taxes accrue to the older generation of pensioners.

Eligibility for social insurance benefits is based on some objective determination that the contingency in question has actually occurred.

For example, the advent of old age is defined as occurring when a person reaches sixty-two or sixty-five. All the claimant needs to establish is proof of identity, age and dependents; the record of earnings that established the benefit level is in the hands of the agency. In most cases, there is little scope for administrative discretion, in contrast to public assistance where discretion necessarily plays a large role.

As a practical matter, however, discretion plays a part in determining eligibility in those segments of the program where a certain amount of judgment is required. Proof of total disability is not as simple to establish as proof of old age. Reasonable men and reasonable physicians can disagree on whether a person in unable 'to engage in any substantial gainful activity by reason of any medically determinable physical or mental impairment.'[5] Unemployment compensation presents complex problems of eligibility determination, since the claimant must show that he was laid off for economic reasons (i.e. made redundant) and did not quit voluntarily or lose his job for disciplinary reasons. Moreover, he must show that he is actively seeking work and willing to accept reasonable job offers. Interpreting the pattern of a claimant's behavior is clearly not the same thing as establishing a fact, and there is ample scope for discretion. The point needs to be made, because in this respect, as in some others, the behavior of the public assistance and the social insurance systems may converge.

In keeping with the motion of an earned right, benefit levels in the social insurance system tend to be earnings-related rather than based on budgetary estimates of family need. This is clearly the case with unemployment compensation in most states. The principle is modified by the presence of minimum and maximum benefits. However, a concept of need enters into the federal programs (Old Age, Survivors' and Disability) and into a few state unemployment insurance programs where benefits also vary by family size.

Perhaps the most important difference between social insurance and public assistance is the absence of the means test in the former. The presence of unearned income or the availability of assets are simply not relevant. Rich or poor are equally entitled, based on their earnings record and subject to the maximum and minimum benefit levels. However, there is a test of earned income, since its presence reduces or eliminates eligibility. This leads to a certain amount of preoccupation with the problem of chiseling, something that the social insurance system shares with its public assistance counterpart.

In contrast to social insurance, public assistance in the United States implies no rights. It maintains the tradition of private charity in that claimants must show that they lack any means of support

from any legally defined source. Thus, the claimant must be someone who has no income or assets. Furthermore, the claimant must
show that no one is available who is legally responsible for his maintenance and whose means are sufficient to contribute to the claimant's support. In the United States, as in Britain, the range of persons
in the kinship group who are economically responsible for one another
has shrunk over the years. Today, responsibility is generally limited to
parents for minor children, and husbands for wives.

It can be noted at this point that both social insurance and public
assistance serve to socialize the burden of supporting the dependent
population by shifting it from kinship lines to a larger body of taxpayers. In this sense, the beneficiaries are not only the claimants, but
also the family members who might otherwise contribute to their
support. This is consonant with the social needs generated by the
decline of the extended family, although the reasons for the reform
came from the problem that the kin of poor claimants were likely to
be poor. The changes in the nature and composition of the nuclear
family that are now in process also present problems to the benefit
structure of aid systems. The American system was certainly based on
the notion that most families are permanent liaisons of husband and
wife who jointly rear their own children; widowhood, desertion,
illegitimacy, and serial polygamy were thought of as deviations that
created economic need in only a relatively insignificant proportion
of the population. The times, however, are changing.

Since the claimant's means are at issue. public assistance programs
have always been characterized by a means test. Benefit levels are
based more specifically on some social minimum estimate of family
need largely determined by family size and composition. Originally,
and ideally in terms of the classic concept, each case's need was
separately evaluated within the framework for the social minimum.
Assistance was rendered not only in cash but with a program of
services designed in the hope that the claimant would be enabled to
improve his lot and reduce or eliminate his claims on the public
purse. However, problems of equity and administrative convenience
led to the creation of standards of need by family size and composition. The Social Security Act of 1935, which created the federally
subsidized public assistance programs, required each state to establish a standard of need. The Act does not require any state to pay
100 per cent of this standard and a number of states actually pay
less than their own standards of need.

Benefits can be high relative to earnings for people in low-wage
labor markets, since benefits are a function of family size and need,
whereas earnings are not related to these factors. Not surprisingly,
rationing devices have developed to concentrate benefits and to con-

fine them to persons who fit some social judgment of being 'needy'. The public assistance tradition in the United States, historically, has been to exclude able-bodied persons who are potentially capable of earning income. This includes single adults, families without minor children, and families with a male head of household. The tradition is not iron-clad, and has been modified in a variety of ways. Virtually all states and localities have provisions for temporary or emergency aid, called General Assistance. GA, as it is known, stands outside the structure of federally subsidized programs. In some states, it can be used for long-term aid, and a few places, such as New York City, use it to supplement low-wage-earning families. About half the states afford aid to intact families with an unemployed male head of household who is not eligible for unemployment insurance. The program is called AFDC–UP (Aid to Families with Dependent Children–Unemployed Parent) and is offered under very restrictive circumstances.

Stigma, administrative restriction, general hassling, and even harassment (in some areas) also play roles as rationing devices. They serve to reduce the number of claimants and their benefits by inducing potential beneficiaries to seek work at earnings below the welfare benefit level, or to obtain help from persons who are not legally responsible for them, or to live below the welfare standard if some other minimal means are, in practice, available to them. Stigma is less of a policy tool than a matter of individual and social perception. As for the administrative practices, their use as rationing devices varies from jurisdiction to jurisdiction. The practices range from the relative permissive standards that are likely to be found in the central cities of the northern industrial states to palpably illegal actions encountered in agricultural areas, especially in the American South.

All income transfer systems that are means tested raise questions of administrative power. The more discretionary the system is, the more power it places in the hands of individual administrators who may use it in an arbitrary and capricious manner. The point has been raised in a variety of ways, ranging from the belief of Piven and Cloward that the intent of welfare is to regulate the behavior of the poor as a group[6] to the widespread concern for the civil liberties of welfare recipients expressed both by partisans such as the National Welfare Rights Organization[7] and by disinterested observers. Emphasis on labor market participation easily translates into administrative coercion. Where administrative coercion is 'proper', i.e. consists of a fair interpretation of the rules, it substitutes for the coercion of the labor market as a form of social control. The smaller the scope for using incentives, the greater will be the reliance on coercion. Thus, hassling the client predictably becomes a policy tool.

The 'crisis' in welfare has become something of a household word in the United States. Most crises pass, in that the problem either gets solved, solves itself, or passes from public consciousness as the public becomes accustomed to a new state of affairs. The present debate over welfare payments is ending its first decade on a well sustained note of hysteria, and a never-failing sense of urgency. What was considered in the 1940s and 1950s as a small set of public charitable programs is now viewed by members of the public as a social problem. People have been known to condemn life in the central city because of the pollution, the crime, *and the welfare,* as if what was once an attempt to solve a social problem has now become a social dysfunction.

The focal point of the crisis consists of beneficiaries who are 'able-bodied', i.e. men and women who are capable of working. There has been little debate over the desirability of helping the aged poor, or the poor in the other 'adult' categories. The aged, the blind, and the disabled have been treated as if they were supposed to be out of the labor market or, at least, as if labor market participation were entirely optional to them. The fact that a good many poor persons who are aged, blind or disabled can work (and often want to work) has been recognized in recent years, and is reflected in the negative tax provisions of the new Supplemental Security Income System. There is, however, little overt pressure to get them into the labor market. The same was never true for adults of working age, except for mothers who were caring for children. And this is where the change in attitude has occurred.

In the first two decades of its existence, the AFDC program was barely noticeable on the American scene. A sharp growth in the number of cases became noticeable in the early 1960s, and quickly became a matter of political concern. The number of cases grew from 800,000 in 1960 to 2·5 million in 1970, an increase of 310 per cent in a ten-year period. Each year saw an increase in the relative as well as the absolute number of recipients. By the end of the decade, the 'crisis' was seemingly permanent. The problem, if defined as too many families on relief, did not pass from the consciousness of the public, despite the fact that the total budgetary costs of the cash programs never exceeded 5 per cent of all government expenditures. Even in impacted cities the financial burden, although not trivial, was far from unbearable. In New York, famed for the size of its welfare population, only 10 per cent of local tax dollars in

B

1971 went to public assistance, including the adult categories that have now been shifted to the Supplemental Security Income Program.[8]

Not only did the AFDC case-load rise sharply, it did so during a decade of almost unparalleled economic growth and prosperity, a period when the proportion of families living in poverty declined from 22 per cent to 12 per cent of the population. A number of explanations have been given for this puzzling phenomenon.

One explanation lies in the increases in benefit level that occurred over the period, which made more persons potentially eligible for benefits. The average monthly AFDC payment rose from $28 to $50 per month between 1960 and 1970. Part of the rise came as various states raised benefit levels, and part of the rise came from the migration that shifted potential welfare recipients from low-benefit states with strict standards of eligibility to high-benefit states with liberal administrative practices. The rise in benefits was greater than the rise in wage levels during the period. Although this had the beneficial effect of raising the abysmal living standards of welfare recipients, it also increased the opportunity cost of working and of keeping a family intact. This situation was more a reflection of the low wage levels available to the unskilled than of the generosity of benefits. It is wrong to attribute all family instability at the poverty level to the effect of welfare benefits that rise relative to wage alternatives. The sociology of ghetto life is complex, but it is certainly safe to say that the benefit–wage effect did not help to strengthen family ties, and was probably a contributing factor to their weakening.[9]

A second explanation for the rise in recipients deals with the administrative changes that were said to have made it easier for applicants to qualify for welfare payments and to remain in receipt of them. A variety of hypotheses has been offered, including suggestions that easier welfare payments were a response to urban rioting, that case-workers were being radicalized, or that the combination of civil rights and welfare rights pressures succeeded in extending access to welfare to more and more people. If income of female-headed households is a rough measure of eligibility, then there is reason to believe that the welfare system had failed, at the beginning of the 1960s, to pick up a lot of eligibles.[10] The increase that occurred was therefore partly a matter of more efficient service to needy people.

The labor market also yielded possible explanations of the sharp rise. Notwithstanding the decline in unemployment during the decade, there was an actual erosion of employment opportunities for the uneducated and unskilled. Much of the decline in the unemployment rate of men with low levels of education stemmed from a decline in the group's labor force participation rate rather than from a rise in its employment. Killingsworth has calculated that the US economy generated a net increase of 10·5 million new jobs for men between 1962 and 1969, but that the upper two-thirds of the male labor force got 13·4 million new jobs, while the lower third *lost* about 3 million. Labor markets at the lower level were characterized by scarcity, discouragement, and declining relative earnings. This situation probably contributed to the rising welfare case-loads at a time when measured unemployment rates were falling.[11]

A number of political issues developed with the rise in the number of able-bodied welfare recipients. One was a taxpayers' revolt in the face of what has been perceived to be a growing 'welfare burden'. Since welfare is administered at the state or local level, people see it as competing for funds with other local activities. Rising and regressive state and local taxes have made themselves felt in taxpayers' pocketbooks. It is safe to say that welfare expenditures are viewed by American taxpayers as being made for an inferior social good when compared with such other outlays as education, police, and public transportation. The squeeze on state and local budgets that developed in 1970–2 was translated, in part, into cuts in welfare benefits and in a tightening of administrative procedures.

This restrictive behavior was predictable from the behavior of the welfare system even during the early 1960s when public attitudes toward the poor were still favorable.[12] Since welfare policy decisions are made at the state and local level, the voters' unfavorable comparisons of welfare outlays with other public expenditures were inevitable.

There is a second level at which the presence of employable adult welfare recipients presents a political problem, and that is where the welfare system creates inequities between welfare recipients and lower-income workers. And it is a potent problem, indeed.

If benefit levels are close to or greater than the after-tax earned income of workers, then horizontal inequities can be considerable, and are likely to find political expression. Leisure is a scarce resource and a valuable commodity. People who must work to support a non-luxurious living standard and who have, let us say, a working spouse, expect that publicly supported leisure should be maintained at a sufficiently low living standard so that the taxpaying workers feel compensated for their forgone leisure.[13] Since this would, in some cases, put welfare living standards at socially impossible low levels, there has always been a certain amount of political tension here. The balancing variable seems to be the stigma of welfare dependency that serves to depress the utility of welfare income below the utility of earned income.

The matter is complicated when welfare incomes rise above earned incomes. The British solution to this problem has been the wage stop by which Supplementary Benefits to the unemployed cannot exceed their usual wage. Wage stop has never been adopted in the United States, and it would present enormous problems in its application to mothers with dependent children – note that the British do not apply it to this group on the presumption that there is no social or political necessity for the mother to go to work. Since there are low-wage labor markets in the United States, there are workers who find themselves earning less at work than they would receive on welfare. Furthermore, since the choice between work and welfare is not a free one, it is often impossible, or at least costly, for a family to make the shift from low-wage employment to welfare.

AFDC might receive less emphasis in American policy debates if the welfare structure provided categories for other prime-age adults. If relief provisions on the same basis were made for other unemployed persons, as is the case in Britain, the distribution of the case-load would not be so peculiarly skewed in the direction of women with children. These, however, are the visible clients of the system, and are therefore the direct objects of policy change. The missing fathers, by the nature of their absence, escape observation and social control.

The Growing Emphasis on Work: the 1967 Amendments

The 1962 amendments to the Social Security Act sought to extend aid and social services to the AFDC clientele by increasing the social work facilities available to them. Whether the approach would have been useful even in a stable situation is doubtful,[14] especially if a reduction in the case-load was the political measure of success. But case-loads continued to soar, and the attempt to apply the small-scale private charity case-work method to the large-scale operations of a municipal welfare department was futile. It is not astonishing that the next round of reform, the 1967 amendments, put stress on getting the mothers into the labor market. If one could not deal with the fathers, if other relatives were exempted, and if case-work would not enable the mothers to be self-supporting then – logically speaking – there was no other method for reducing the case-load than to get the mothers into the labor market.

The 1967 amendments marked a considerable shift in attitude toward the employability of mothers who were heads of households. The founders of the Social Security Act had viewed the mother as a homebody (and an unwelcome competitor in the labor market) and the subsequent extension of social insurance to widows of workers caring for children reflected a similar view. Rural southern welfare departments never shared this attitude, and even urban northern welfare departments kept a work requirement of sorts in the regulation books. However, the rising labor force participation rate of women, including married women with children of school age, made the working mother a commonplace spectacle on the American scene. By 1973, some 41 per cent of all children had mothers in the labor force.[15] As a result, the idea that a mother's socially proper place was at home, rearing children, became increasingly foreign. If going to work was good enough for the working class mother, then it certainly seemed good enough for her poorer sister.

This became the new social judgment. It reflected itself in legislative debates, in the 1967 amendments, and in subsequent legislation.

The welfare tradition in the United States was never intended to deal with the able-bodied at all, except to give temporary help. The unsupported mothers were a federal category because mothers, in 1935, were not fully able-bodied in the labor market sense of the term. The fact that many worked anyway was a reflection both of the low benefit levels and of the powerful stigma attached to the receipt of welfare. Although the Great Depression made both the states and the federal government into purveyors of public assistance, the notion that this was more than an emergency measure was fiercely resisted by all levels of government. Most of the aid that was offered was work relief or job creation. The only social insurance program for the able-bodied that came out of the Depression was Unemployment Insurance. This offered temporary succor to men and women who had 'earned' it through their previous work, and required beneficiaries to look for work. Indeed, all income maintenace programs for able-bodied persons have been run on the proposition that such persons have an obligation to support themselves and their dependents. A program that would sustain a work-eligible person indefinitely seems culturally and politically inconceivable in the United States at the present time.

What happened to the welfare mothers around 1967 was that they were promoted to the ranks of the able-bodied, and attitudes toward the able-bodied were applied to them. To some extent these attitudes hardened in the late 1960s and early 1970s when the boom of the 1960s came to an end. I have argued elsewhere that the slower the rate of economic growth, the harder the choice between public and private goods. As public goods become relatively more costly, social priorities are reordered. Helping poor people of working age is likely to rank low under such circumstances.[16]

Work Incentives in AFDC
As noted earlier, the 1967 changes in the law introduced financial incentives to female AFDC recipients to earn income on the labor market. Claimants who found work were permitted to retain their

working expenses and the first $30 per month of earnings before loss of benefits occurred. In addition, they could keep one-third of the rest of their earnings. It is noteworthy that Congress did not intend to create thereby an income supplement generally available to low-income families. The benefit was restricted to persons who found work after having been welfare recipients for at least four months, and who had not refused suitable work or quit their jobs in order to qualify. In the twenty-three states that offer AFDC benefits to unemployed male heads of families (AFDC–UP), the incentive is restricted to taking part-time jobs, since working more than 100 hours in a month disqualifies the male from *any* benefit.

Congress did not rely on financial incentives alone, and made it compulsory for AFDC recipients to register in a manpower program called the Work Incentive Program (WIN), which will be described further on. The incentive has undoubtedly had an effect on the work behavior of welfare mothers.[17] Sixteen per cent of the caseload was working in 1973, up from 14 per cent in 1967 and 1969. Part of the increase undoubtedly reflects an accumulation effect, since the working recipient's income would have to rise substantially before she became totally disqualified from benefits.

AFDC has also become a passport to other benefits, such as free school lunches, preferential access to day care, Medicaid (immensely important in states where eligibility is restricted to public assistance claimants), and preferential access to public housing, where this is available. In addition, food stamps are easier to obtain since being on welfare is *prima facie* evidence of eligibility.[18]

At first glance, it would appear that working AFDC recipients face an implicit marginal tax rate of 66⅔ per cent on earnings past the disregarded work expenses and $30 per month, that is, 66⅔ cents in benefits are lost for every additional dollar earned. However, since the other benefits are also income-conditioned, marginal tax rates on earnings can run past the 100 per cent mark. In the United States, this phenomenon is called the 'notch problem'. British readers will recognize it as the 'poverty trap'. In the AFDC context it might better be described as a 'welfare trap' : earnings opportunities available to mothers in the poverty population are generally not high enough to get them off welfare. The work incentive serves not to reduce the number of recipients, as was the aim of Congress, but to increase their numbers and the length of their stay on the rolls.

The structure of the work incentive creates a number of inequities and anomalies among similarly situated members of the population. Male-headed families are at a disadvantage to female-headed ones, since work in excess of 100 hours disqualifies the male recipient. This maintains the incentives to families to split up, something that Congress sought to blunt in 1962 by making males eligible (in participating states) for AFDC–UP. There are great state-to-state variations in the way that work expenses are defined, a seemingly minor detail that significantly changes the amount of earnings retained by the claimant. Finally, low-wage-earners who are not receiving benefits have substantially lower net incomes than claimants, but cannot obtain benefits without passing through a four-month period of unemployment.

MANPOWER POLICY IN THE USA

The increasing emphasis on labor market participation by the welfare dependent population raises issues in manpower policy. The population at risk contains persons who not only are handicapped by past and present racial discrimination, but also suffer from a lack of skills that are salable on the labour market. Presumably, it is a task of manpower policy to address itself to the latter problem.

The US government's first major step into a manpower policy came with the passage of the Manpower Development and Training Act (MDTA) of 1962. A major purpose of this Act was economic rather than social : to facilitate economic growth and to help make compatible two seemingly incompatible goals, low unemployment and price stability. Manpower training was seen as a cure for structural unemployment. Hence, the early training programs focused on experienced workers whose skills were obsolete, but who were otherwise capable of competing in labor markets. Helping to upgrade the skills of socially disadvantaged workers was a lesser objective, and training of the welfare-dependent poor was a minor aspect of the operation.

The low rates of unemployment in primary labor markets during the mid- and late 1960s led to a change in the emphasis of manpower policy. Focus shifted to helping the disadvantaged. The structure of programs that developed was decentralized in 1973 by the Comprehensive Employment and Training Act (CETA). The new law places primary responsibility for the planning and execution of programs in state and local governments, called prime sponsors. These, in turn, can make contracts with private or public agencies to get the actual training done. The federal government finances the programs through a revenue-sharing process, and lends technical assistance to the prime sponsors. The new legislation assumes that states and localities are better judges of their own needs than the distant federal government; in addition, mayors and governors prefer to have some control over expenditures made within their bailiwicks.

Notwithstanding the above change, manpower policy is not likely to alter drastically within the next few years,[19] although there may be shifts of emphasis. Thus, it may be profitable to review the major manpower training programs that evolved in the pre-CETA years, since they are still more or less in effect in their decentralized forms.

MDTA Programs

The two programs associated with the original 1962 Act were Institutional Training and On-the-Job Training. The former was conducted in classrooms and other off-site facilities. The latter provided supervised work on the job sites of private employers who received compensation for their training expenses and damages to equipment. Employers had the right of refusal to accept trainees referred to them. Both programs provided training allowances for unemployed trainees, but not for new entrants into the labor market unless they were poor youth between the ages of seventeen and twenty-one. After 1966, MDTA programs were required to enroll at least 65 per cent of trainees from among disadvantaged groups, e.g. blacks, Hispanics and others.

Job Opportunities in the Business Sector

Job Opportunities in the Business Sector (JOBS) was aimed at the long-term unemployed with special emphasis on racial minorities. Co-administered by the Manpower Administration and the National Alliance of Businessmen, the program contracted with private firms to train workers and to provide them with work experience. Trainees were paid by the employer, whose contract with JOBS provided for costs and a reasonable profit. An intent of the program was to induce employers to hire some of their trainees, but little information exists as to the extent of this practice. Since the bulk of the jobs have been relatively low-wage entry jobs, it is likely that JOBS also behaves like a subsidized employment program.

Job Corps

The target population for this program was poverty-stricken young persons who left school before completing their secondary education. Job Corps centers have been operated by various private and public organizations, and have offered remedial education, counseling, and skill development. The training allowances are structured to provide an incentive to the trainee to complete the course. A purpose of the program has been to remove trainees from their environment. Accordingly, Job Corps participants live away from home in centers operated by the program.

Neighborhood Youth Corps

Neighborhood Youth Corps addresses itself to poor youth who were potential or actual school drop-outs. As indicated by the name, it recruits on a neighborhood basis and its clients live at home. The largest part of the program has been summer work, intended not only to give work experience during the non-school months, but also to provide income to disadvantaged youth and keep them from being idle. Undoubtedly, the program was inspired by the urban riots in the United States in the mid-1960s. On a smaller scale, NYC has provided an in-school program of part-time jobs. On the whole, NYC has come closer to being an income maintenance program, with some work attached, than to being a training program.

Work Incentive Program

The Work Incentive Program, as mentioned earlier, is specifically directed at recipients of public assistance, and remains a federal program not encompassed by CETA. One of its major functions is to serve as the work test for claimants, since all adult AFDC recipients must register. However, most are unaffected by the program. Only 29 per cent of adult beneficiaries were 'participants' of the program in 1973, the balance having either been rejected or not even screened. Emphasis has shifted from training to placement (the present program is called WIN II to distinguish it from its predecessor), and a subsidy is offered to employers who hire WIN participants.

Public Employment Program

The Public Employment Program is clearly a job creation program with an income maintenance function, and there is no special training component involved. Strictly speaking, PEP is not a permanent part of the manpower structure, although it is usually listed along with other manpower programs. Created by the Emergency Employment Act in 1971 to help alleviate the high unemployment problem of that year, it was revived in 1974 and 1975 because of the extraordinarily high levels of unemployment of that time. PEP seems likely to persist as long as American unemployment rates remain high, and thus to serve as a substitute form of (or alternative to) public assistance.

As can be seen from the above, job creation and income maintenance functions are mixed with rehabilitation, training and placement. In this respect, the American approach differs substantially from the British and from other European manpower policies that focus on the training and placement functions, and leave income maintenance and rehabilitation to be dealt with separately by the social service agencies of government. The American approach reflects that relatively high levels of unemployment that prevailed in the United States, as compared with Europe, even during the boom years of the late 1960s, and the concentration of this unemployment among the black and Spanish minorities. It also helps fill the gaps in the American income maintenance system, whereby able-bodied persons except female household heads are largely excluded from public assistance.

SUMMARY

In the United States, the Social Security Act created a social insurance system and kept it separate from the older notions of public assistance. By and large, public assistance was aimed at people who were not 'eligible' to participate in the labor market, either temporarily or permanently.[20] Exceptions were made here and there, depending on individual circumstances, or on the generosity of local administrators or case-workers. Little or no interrelationships were perceived between public assistance as a form of income maintenance and labor market policies, if any, and the relatively low take-up of public assistance benefits kept the subject from impinging on the American consciousness.

Indeed, the principal recognized labor market policy in the United States was to maintain aggregate demand at full employment, subject to the constraint of relatively stable prices. This was the intent of the Employment Act of 1946. Th policy tools were fiscal policy and, after 1953, monetary policy. Beyond that, government did not really have any set of microeconomic labor market policies and it was assumed that, except for periodic recessions (or 'rolling readjustments'), anyone who needed a job could get one. The Manpower Development and Training Act (MDTA) of 1961 marked a major departure from that view. The growth and crisis of the welfare system in the 1960s occurred at the same time that manpower training established itself as a labor market policy to aid workers who needed to retrain or upgrade their skills. As time passed, a greater role for training developed in public assistance. This raised a number of labor market issues. Among such issues were the relationship of wages to benefit levels, implicit tax rates of benefit systems, work incentives, impact of benefit programs on family structure, and similar manifestations of an interactive system. The issue remains troublesome because of its complexity. Since the American experience is not necessarily unique, comparison with the British system may be fruitful for both countries.

Great Britain has welfare programs that are generous relative to the wage alternatives open to unskilled persons. In addition, Great Britain has an active manpower policy that is more highly organized than the American. It may help to gain some perspective on the American problem if we examine parallel phenomena in Britain. The basis for the comparison is laid in the next chapter. A listing of the major British and American benefits relevant to prime age adults is given in the Appendix to Chapter 2.

3 A Comparative View

THE BASIS FOR COMPARING BRITAIN AND THE USA
Fruitful comparison between Great Britain and the United States may be made for a number of reasons. To begin with, Britain[1] and the United States have some common historical traditions with respect to work and welfare, and these traditions are reflected in current policies and practices. There is a strong work ethic in Britain that antedates and was reinforced by the Protestant reformation. This ethic manifests itself in the stigma that attaches to welfare dependency, although the stigma is probably not so great in Britain as in the United States. It is not that the British – or at least, the English – are passionately devoted to work as an end in itself, as has been said of Germans or Japanese. Leisure is a highly valued commodity, but income from work has a higher status than income from welfare for persons below the pensionable age. However, income from property has an even higher status.

One phenomenon common to both countries is the steady rise in the number of female household heads (or unsupported mothers) who receive public assistance benefits (see Figure 3.1). Americans have viewed this as a sort of social catastrophe. It is not considered to be a great problem in Britain, although a certain amount of uneasiness on the subject can be detected beneath the surface.[2] Strictly speaking, an unsupported mother in Britain has no legal obligation whatsoever to seek work. She is free to collect her Supplementary Benefit until the last child is sixteen years old. However, complaints by welfare rights groups that welfare mothers are being harassed into work are some indication that the social values of some administrators differ from the official judgment that the fatherless household without adequate means has an unqualified legal right to public support.

Some of the similarity in attitude towards public assistance can be attributed to the common descent of both the British and the American system from the Elizabethan Poor Law. Strictly speaking, the term 'Poor Law' was abolished in the 1948 reform. Public assistance was called National Assistance (NA) until 1966, when its

FIGURE 3.1 Comparative Growth of Public Assistance Case-Loads, 1961–73 : Mothers with Dependent Children

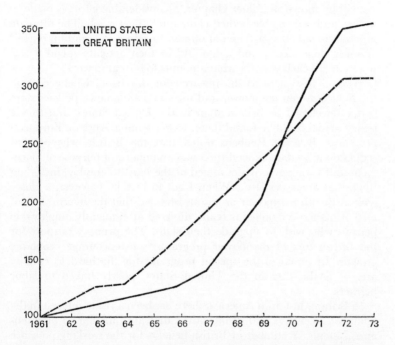

Source: Computed from data on British women under sixty with dependent children receiving supplementary benefit. Department of Health and Social Security, *Social Security Statistics: 1973* (London: HMSO, 1974). The American data are based on the AFDC case-load. US Department of Health, Education and Welfare, *Social Security Bulletin: Annual Statistical Supplement, 1973* (Washington: US Government Printing Office, 1974).

name was changed to Supplementary Benefits (SB). The change in terminology was made by the Labour government in an effort to destigmatize the benefits. The implication is that SB merely supplements the existing National Insurance benefits which, like all social insurance benefits, are not means-tested. As a practical matter, SB retains a strong concern for work, notwithstanding its innocuous title. As will be shown in a later chapter, a considerable effort is made to induce and coerce able-bodied claimants[3] to get a job. The ultimate sanction is jail. It is a criminal offense to refuse to maintain oneself or one's dependents, and a handful of men actually spend a few weeks in jail each year for what amounts to refusal to work.

When I first planned the research for this book, I believed that the links between manpower and income maintenance policies were better developed in Britain than in the United States, and that a policy model could be found there. In her seminal work on European programs, Beatrice Reubens noted that the British believed that reduction in welfare expenditures was an important purpose of placement and training activities aimed at the hard to employ, including those that are 'work-shy'.[4] When I got to Britain, however, a closer look at British manpower programs revealed that the mainstream of formal manpower policy is really directed at eminently employable persons who wish to upgrade their skills. The primary purpose for the British mix of manpower programs is to encourage economic growth. In practice, the special programs for the hard to employ are, as is the case in the United States, poorly linked to labor markets.

In Britain, just as in America, there has been a rising interest in the financial incentives and disincentives that are inherent in maintenance systems. A number of British benefits for the working poor are keyed to income; some have negative tax rates, as in Family Income Supplement (FIS), which pays 50 per cent of the difference between the earnings of a fully employed head of household and a poverty line for a family of his size and composition. Indeed, negative tax legislation, called Tax Credits, might have been enacted if it were not for the precipitous fall of the Conservative government in 1974.

Similarity of Economic Problems
Comparisons between Britain and America are further facilitated by the existence of a number of similar problems. Among these are relatively high levels of unemployment, at least by European standards, together with chronic balance of payments problems that limit the scope of full employment policy. There is also a variety of structural imperfections in the labor market that bear resemblance

to some found in the United States. Similarity does not, of course, imply identity. Some labor market problems in Britain are quite different from America's but the similar ones are worth looking at in some small detail.

Unemployment. Britain has a greater political commitment to full employment than the United States. However, the British have suffered from unemployment rates that are consistently higher than those found in the advanced industrial countries of western Europe, excepting Italy (see Figure 3.2). By the same token, the peacetime unemployment rate in the United States has not been sustainable at a rate below 5 per cent without loss of price stability. Although it has been widely believed in America that cyclical unemployment does not have much influence on case-loads, new evidence is emerging that a relationship does exist.[5]

Some of the unemployment that both nations have experienced comes from structural problems and other labor market imperfections that do not lend themselves to treatment by the usual macroeconomic policies to stimulate demand. (Even in this respect, both nations have faced similar constraints on demand stimulation that come from balance of payments problems.) As in the United States, Britain has depressed areas, notably in the Southwest and North of England and in Wales and Scotland. Another similarity to the United States is found in the underinvestment in human capital among a segment of the population. Racial and ethnic problems also manifest themselves in the labor market, both on the demand side through discriminatory hiring practices, and on the supply side through lack of skills and through cultural deprivation. Unfortunately, there is relatively little statistical information available on race and ethnicity in Britain, even though race problems are quite acute. No data exist on claimants to most benefits by race or ethnicity,[6] and very few data are available on anything else pertaining to race. This situation is now being corrected with the gathering of some statistical series based on place of birth and parents' place of birth. These are census categories, but they also identify race.[7]

Differences between Britain and the USA

The similarities in some labor market and other problems that invite comparison have been noted above. However, there are important differences that must be stressed in any comparative analysis, for the common language tends to disguise (at least for the casual visitor) some substantial differences between Britain and America.

Unemployment. Although levels of unemployment have been high by the standards that have prevailed in western Europe, they have generally been low when compared to the United States. In the

FIGURE 3.2 Average Annual Unemployment Rates in Selected Countries, Adapted to US Concepts, 1962–74

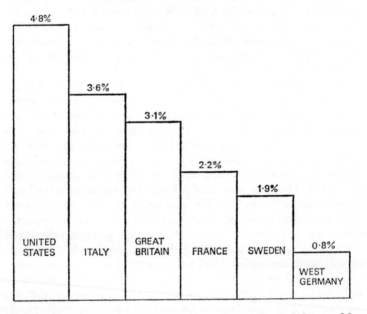

Source: Computed from data in Constance Sorrentino and Joanna Moy, 'Unemployment in Nine Industrialized Countries', *Monthly Labor Review,* vol. 98, no. 6 (June 1975) pp. 9–18.

decade of the 1960s the rate of unemployment in Great Britain, when adjusted for comparability with the United States, ranged from a low of 2·1 per cent to a high of 4 per cent. Even the 1972 rate, which was the highest since World War II, only reached 4·3 per cent.[8] By contrast, the US unemployment rate in the 1960s ranged from 3.5 per cent to 6·7 per cent, climbing to close to 9 per cent in 1975 (as compared with 3·6 per cent in Great Britain). It is widely believed that the low rates in America cannot be sustained without inflation. If we distinguish between the income maintenance and productive systems of an economy,[9] there has been relatively more room for people in the productive system in Britain than in America. The obverse of this coin can be found in the relatively low wages and living standards found in Great Britain. Thus, an average male wage-earner in manufacturing earned £41·52 per week in 1973. Given an exchange rate of £1 = $2·40 this comes to $104 per week as compared (roughly) with $165 for his counterpart in the United States.[10]

Arguably, the less productive British economy is able to employ relatively more people, at lower wages, and thus puts less pressure on the income maintenance system to correct undesirable shortfalls, at least with respect to the population of working age. If poverty is viewed as a nationally relative concept, then the greater equality in the income distribution makes poverty in Britain a somewhat less acute matter than in America. At the same time, it brings the socially acceptable minimum level of income closer to the average. The socially acceptable minimum income in an advanced industrial country is probably affected by the living standards in neighboring countries with which much of the population and most of its elites have contact. Standards of living in most of western Europe are higher than in Britain. The result is a squeeze between wage opportunities and the social minimum income as defined, in Britain, by the level of Supplementary Benefits. A low-wage-earner (say, one who earns two-thirds of average earnings if fully employed) with a wife and two children who qualifies for SB could receive 82 per cent of his earnings in benefits if not at work. With four children, the SB payment would be close to 100 per cent.[11]

CULTURAL AND POLITICAL ATTITUDES

An important difference between the United States and Britain can be found in attitudes toward the role of women, and concern for the welfare of children (as well as for the aged and others incapable of working). British women have about the same labor force participation rate as their US counterparts but, to the casual observer, older cultural norms prevail with respect to attitude. That woman's place is in the home is still something of a British ideal (at least, for men) which is, perforce, honored in the breach. This translates into less political pressure to send poor women to work than is found in the United States or even on the continent of Europe. For example, SB is relatively gentle with middle-aged widows (as compared with the United States) who have had a career as housewives. As for women who are caring for dependent children, their right to assistance is unqualified.

The attitude toward mothers with children also seems a function of a strong British compassionate streak for children. Whether or not adult poverty is well deserved, children are never thought to be at fault. They did not chose their parents, nor are they in any position to alter their own circumstance. Child poverty seems particularly abhorrent to the British (possibly more so than to Americans). Perhaps this is a hangover from the harsh attitudes that prevailed in Britain in the nineteenth century. Whatever the reason, both major political parties have a traditional concern for child welfare. Not surprisingly, the principal lobbying group for the poor is called the Child Poverty Action Group (CPAG).

One reflection of this concern for children is shown in Family Allowances (FAM). FAM is payable to all families with two or more children, at the weekly rate of 90 pence for the second child and £1 for each additional child. More to the point, FAM is payable directly to the mother, on the hypothesis that she, more than the father, has the child's welfare at heart. Hence, FAM is more than just a redistribution of income toward families with children, as might be the case in France or Canada.

A 1968 change in FAM sought to concentrate the benefits of increased payments on poor families. It did this through 'claw-back', a device by which a 50 pence increase in benefits was just offset by an equivalent reduction in the portion of income that is free of taxes. Since FAM is taxable, the full benefit of the increase went to families whose incomes were low enough to place them below the tax threshhold.[12]

The Family Income Supplement Program (FIS) was a further attempt, this time by a Conservative government, to help low-wage families with children. Eligibility for this wage supplement (see the Appendix to this chapter) hinges on the presence of children in a low-wage household. FIS was enacted in response to a perceived political demand to help poor children, and was a Tory substitute for a broader and more universal Family Allowance program proposed by the Labour Party. The Tory measure reflected a political need to respond to Labour demands for broadened family allowances, i.e. an income maintenance measure focused on children.

If there can be such a thing as a poverty lobby, its political strength is relatively greater in Britain than in the United States. Some of this strength comes from what Americans would call the welfare establishment, i.e. social workers and social planners in public and private agencies as well as in academia. The late Professor Richard Titmuss was a strong influence on this group, in so far as he developed social administration as the academic field of study from which the relevant experts are drawn. Not only did he build it up to its present importance in Britain, but he also imprinted it with his political views and analytical methods, especially the notion that a primary function of the welfare state is to help people who are in need. The tradition survives in the students and disciples that he produced for several decades at the London School of Economics, and it would be difficult today to appoint a distinguished panel of British experts without naming one of Titmuss's co-workers or students. There is no comparably unified intellectual force in social welfare in the United States, although American schools of social work probably have somewhat parallel views.

In general, the 'socialism' of the British welfare state puts heavier emphasis on distributive justice than on economic growth as the means toward a better society. This differs from the US emphasis on economic growth as the basic way to reduce poverty.

A comparison between the United States and Great Britain must also note the somewhat different role of cash relief in the panoply of social welfare benefits. Since everyone in Britain has access to the National Health Service, there is no need to qualify for welfare in order to obtain health benefits (except for free prescriptions, eye glasses, and dental care). Family Allowances are not means-tested. Public housing is not designed, as in the United States, for the very poorest, but serves a broad spectrum of working class people, reaching well into the middle income ranges. There is also a variety of means-tested benefits that do not require total poverty as the principal qualification of eligibility. Among these are free school meals, rent rebates, and other benefits available to the working poor. Some of these, like rent rebates or FAM, are not additive to SB, and thus shift some of the expense away from the SB budget. This puts a slightly lesser burden of the total cost of income maintenance on the formal public assistance system. Furthermore, although SB *is* a passport to the many means-tested benefits available in Britain, it is not the exclusive one. FIS also serves this function. Accordingly, there is a lesser need for persons in search of one particular benefit to try to qualify for the whole package – including SB – in order to obtain the benefit. Unbundling is easier.

There are other major differences in the role of SB, as compared to Aid to Families with Dependent Children, which will be noted here for further development in a later chapter. SB is a broader program in that it covers intact families, and in that it *supplements* social insurance benefits that fall short of British minimum social standards. In this respect, it covers a larger pool of potentially eligible people than its American counterpart. The political consequence is that a larger proportion of working people in Britain are likely to have at least potential contact with public assistance than is the case in America where, for most people, AFDC is something for 'them' and not for 'us'. Accordingly, the attitude of the British electorate can be expected to be more benign toward public assistance because of the greater likelihood that the ordinary voter will have occasion to use it.

The foregoing establishes a basis for comparing Britain with the United States in so far as problems of income maintenance for able-bodied persons is concerned. A reader's guide to welfare benefits in both countries is given in the appendices to Chapters 2 and 3. It is not intended to be complete, but it may be helpful to readers who have not yet been initiated into the mysteries of social welfare programs. The inclusion of training allowances in the list of benefits reflects the idea that training is a relevant alternative to unemployment. In the chapter that follows, a close look will be taken at British social insurance and public assistance, and at the manner in which the various programs interact with each other to create a structure of incentives with respect to the labor market.

4 Britain: The Interplay of Social Insurance and Public Assistance Programs

HISTORICAL BACKGROUND

British income maintenance before World War II was, like its continental counterparts, oriented towards the social insurance principle. This meant linking eligibility with participation in the labor market, and using a fund, preferably contributory, to finance claims. The use of a fund was considered 'sound' among policy-makers who feared any system with an unlimited claim on general tax revenues. The same sort of reasoning underlies American Social Security with its payroll taxes and its trust funds.

By 1939, four funds were in existence in Britain : health insurance, unemployment insurance, agricultural unemployment insurance, and pensions for the aged, widows and orphans. These had been developed over time in a piecemeal way. However, coverage was far from comprehensive, benefits were limited, and administration was was complex and costly. The concept underlying the services was that of making special provision for the minimum requirements of groups that were in particular need.[1]

The backstop program to these funds was public assistance, which was the old Poor Law in its final stage. As in the United States, public assistance was primarily a local matter, although its form and content were mandated to the localities (local authorities) by Parliament. Indigent persons who were not eligible for aid by the funds, and who could not get other aid, were the potential clients of the Poor Law, which served as the net below the safety net.

However, the high levels of unemployment that began in the mid-1920s exhausted the unemployment insurance fund and put strains on public assistance. The Poor Law was not, in any event, designed to help able-bodied workers. The crisis that developed from this situation led to the enactment of a second type of public assistance, called Unemployment Assistance. This was funded out of general revenues and administered by a national board.

The Unemployment Assistance program used the means test to dole out its benefits. In this respect it followed the general principle behind *assistance*, in contrast to social *insurance*. Since the volume of claims on assistance is limited only by circumstance and not by the size of the fund, the need to economize funds requires a rationing device. The means test experience that was developed under the Poor Law seemed most applicable to the situation. Coverage under Unemployment Assistance was quite broad, which gave a far greater proportion of the population some experience with the means test than had been the case with the old Poor Law. As a result, the means test became politically unpopular, a factor that undoubtedly played a role in the post-war reform of British social services.

The Goals of the Beveridge Plan
The formation of the British welfare state after World War II was heavily influenced by the Beveridge Report.[2] One aspect of the reforms coming from the Beveridge Report was that the various patchwork programs were consolidated into one comprehensive system. The backbone of the Beveridge plan for income maintenance was a contributory form of social insurance. Heavy emphasis was placed on the *prevention* of poverty by the use of family allowances, a comprehensive health and rehabilitation service, and by a Keynesian full employment policy. The contributory social insurance benefits were set at subsistence. In a sense, this was all that the state owed the citizen, and Beveridge envisioned the development of private insurance schemes to supplement the basic subsistence benefit for those who might choose this form of saving. Since the social insurance system was contributory, the benefits were clearly a matter of right, earned by the recipient. The stigma of public charity, and the indignity of the means test, were thus to be dispensed with.

There was still a need to provide for those who might be in need but did not qualify by virtue of direct or indirect attachment to the labor market. National Assistance (NA) was to meet this need. In essence, NA was the nationalized form of the locally administered Poor Law, together with the Unemployment Assistance program, pension supplements, and similar odds and ends. In this respect, the public assistance patchwork, like the insurance system, was made comprehensive.

It was believed in Britain, just as in the United States, that public assistance would be a minor part of British social security, especially as time moved the younger generation through full coverage. This did not turn out to be the case, and today the number of persons receiving Supplementary Benefits (the present name for National Assistance) as their primary form of income maintenance is one-third as great as the number of National Insurance beneficiaries.[3]

The actual welfare state that emerged from the post-war reforms differed from the Beveridge blueprint in a number of respects. Of the policies to prevent poverty that were enacted, only the National Health Service emerged in full form. Family Allowances (FAM) never became a great enough income transfer device to bring many people out of poverty. Although a full employment policy was pursued, and kept unemployment below United States levels, it encountered the following interrelated problems : (1) It proceeded on a stop–go basis, since balance of payment problems recurrently forced policy-makers to truncate each boom, and (2) a persistently low rate of real economic growth left relatively little scope for raising real wages for workers in the low-wage sector. Therefore there was little scope for using economic growth to reduce the number of the poor.

Conflict Among the Goals

In the enactment of the operative social security scheme, three basic Beveridge goals came into conflict with each other. One was the proposition that social security benefits should be paid out at a flat rate set at what can be called a social minimum income. The second goal was that all needy families should receive, as a general rule, a social minimum level of income. The third was that social insurance benefits should somehow be felt to be preferable to assistance benefits.[4]

If assistance were felt as less desirable than insurance, one would have expected it to offer lower benefits. But this was not the case, since both were supposedly set at a 'minimum' level. Furthermore, national insurance benefits tended to fall below assistance benefits when rent and other variables were taken into consideration. Since national assistance was used to supplement national insurance if the latter benefits fell below the minimum, some proportion of national insurance claimants were always entitled to national assistance. These, it should be noted had fulfilled their side of the social bargain, in that they had directly or indirectly 'earned' their benefits. At the same time, the policy that a minimum benefit was available to all in need removed the economic difference to the claimants between the two programs. There remained, of course, the indignity of the means test and the stigma of charity with respect to assistance, but this was blunted by the presence of claimants with overlapping coverage.

If the assistance benefit levels represented the society's calculation of a minimum standard of living, then the insurance benefits could, by themselves, be economically less desirable even if 'morally superior'. The goal of setting social insurance benefits at a flat subsistence was not achieved. At the same time, it was difficult to assert that the insurance benefits were somehow more desirable when, in fact, they were economically inferior.

There were several separate roads that might have led out of this dilemma, and British policy moved along all of them. One was to keep certain assistance benefits low, a second was to raise the insurance benefits, and the third was to use assistance as a supplement to insurance. Each presented problems, and all of them together served to complicate matters.

It is difficult to assert that everyone ought to be guaranteed some socially determined minimum income while simultaneously deciding that some people should receive benefits below this. Yet, this is what wage stop does. Wage stop is a device that limits the level of assistance benefits to what the principal wage-earner could earn on the labor market. This made national insurance economically preferable to national assistance for disemployed wage-earners in the lowest wage brackets, but at the politically uncomfortable cost of specifying that they were to be supported at a level below the social minimum.

The move to raise insurance benefits, relative to assistance, came via the introduction of earnings-related benefits, first for pensions (1961), and then for unemployment and sickness benefits, (1966). This removed the Beveridge assumption that all benefits would be at some flat-rate basic level. The introduction of earnings-related benefits made it possible for workers to receive benefits above the minimum scale, subject to an upper limit and to the constraint that the combined benefit (basic plus earnings-related) could not exceed 85 per cent of average weekly earnings.[5] In order to maintain the actuarial soundness of the scheme, it was necessary to depart from still another Beveridge notion, the flat-rate contribution, and to add a proportional payroll tax (subject to an upper limit) to the flat rate. Since the point at which the earnings-related benefits comes into play is a low one, the overlap between assistance and insurance has not been removed for much of the working population.

As noted above, it is British policy to supplement inadequate national insurance benefits, and a considerable overlap in coverage exists. Under the circumstances, it has been hard to maintain that one benefit should be felt to be 'less desirable' than the other. This dilemma was resolved when the Ministry of Social Security Act of 1966 moved to destigmatize National Assistance for all claimants.

The program was renamed Supplementary Benefits (SB) and divided into two components : Supplementary Pensions and Supplementary Assistance.[6] Claimants were given an explicit 'right' to benefits, based entirely on the rules of qualification. The purpose of this move (by itself, it made no practical difference) was to remove the mantle of public charity from the assistance benefits. In other words, two of the Beveridge goals gave way to the third and most fundamental goal : the right of all persons in need and unable to work to receive a minimum level of income money.

This must be qualified (somehow, grand principles are never neat) by two provisos : (1) the definition of who is unable to work, i.e. not expected to look for work, and (2) the wage stop. The most important difference between the United States and the British statutory definitions of 'able-bodied' lies in the treatment of female heads of households caring for children, or what the British call unsupported mothers. There is no legal obligation for an unsupported mother to seek work. She is entitled to support from the state at SB levels, although this does not remove the legal liabilities of husbands, fathers, or co-habiting males for her maintenance or the maintenance of the children. The work test is not applied, at least by statute, to unsupported mothers, regardless of whether they are 'able' to work and earn at least the equivalent of the benefit.[7]

Households where an able-bodied male head is incapable of earning the social minimum income on the labor market are not entitled to receive it from SB. This is the qualification to the notion of a social minimum that is introduced by the wage stop. It appears to condemn a portion of the lowest paid population to perpetual sub-poverty – sub-poverty because the SB itself is considered to be a kind of poverty line – in order to maintain a work incentive. For reasons elaborated in the next chapter, the application of wage stop has declined, falling from 12·2 per cent of unemployed SB claimants in 1966 to 4 per cent in 1973.[8]

INTERRELATIONSHIPS : NATIONAL INSURANCE AND
SUPPLEMENTARY BENEFITS

As we have seen above, insurance and assistance are not two separate income maintenance devices with separate clienteles and separate functions. They are sub-systems that interact with each other. The result of the interaction has been to change the role of assistance from the simple one of the 'net below the safety net' into a sub-system of the larger income maintenance system. In the larger system, assistance serves as a supplement to and as a substitute for the other public income transfer schemes, as well as for the income distribution that is carried out through the private sector. It is merely one of a variety of public measures that substitute and supplement (as the case may be) private income, and which service not only to redistribute income in general, but also to shift the burden of income transfers from relatives (and friends) to the taxpayers at large.[9] Public income transfers, where applicable, are a substitute for private ones, although private transfers continue to play a role of unknown dimension as licit and illicit supplements to public transfers. The particular mix of income transfer components that are available to any particular claimant, and the level of support it offers, is much more a matter of circumstance than whether the benefit has been 'earned' (and is thus 'deserved') by the claimant.

This can be seen more clearly if we look at income maintenance by function rather than by program, and since this work concerns the able-bodied, the example might just as well be drawn from unemployment. Ostensibly, the major program in aid of the unemployed is the national insurance system's Unemployment Benefit (UB). It covers workers who have paid the full flat and graduated contribution for at least six months, and who are out of work and looking for work. The benefit lasts for a year at the flat rate, but the earnings-related supplement runs out after six months. Take a household consisting of a working husband earning £36 per week, a nonworking wife, and two children, paying £6 a week in rent. Assume that the combined value of savings and redundancy payments is no greater than £325, which might easily be the case for someone who has been working for less than ten years on a job. Unemployment Benefit, including earnings-related supplement, will be in the neighborhood of £22 per week; add about £3 to this for rent rebate and FAM, and his benefit will amount to about £25, of which £7·57 will have been the earnings-related supplement. If unemployment persists for more than six months, the £7·57 supplement ceases. However, this brings the family below the minimum for supplementary Benefits which, in this case, would be about £25 (including FAM and rent rebate). Since the family is entitled to claim SB, the loss in income is closer to £4 than to £7. This is the true size of the earnings-related supplement in the above case, the rest being a taxation and bookkeeping device.[10]

From the point of view of the family's financial welfare, the change in the administrative mix of income transfer programs is less significant than the fluctuations in family income that the changes entail. In the first six months of the spell of unemployment, the components of the public income transfers to this family would consist of UB, both flat-rate and supplemented, plus FAM for the second child, plus rent rebate. In the second six months, the mix changes somewhat, as part of UB drops out and is replaced, in part, by payments from

SB. Should the unemployment continue past twelve months, the rest of the UB drops out and is replaced by SB, which is calculated net of FAM and the rent rebate.[11]

Just to spell out this mix of benefits, and the changes in the mix that can occur is to underscore the proposition that public assistance (SB) is merely one of a set of benefits rather than a separate program. Hence, SB in Britain has passed the point where it is residual, except in the administrative sense. It follows that the 1966 legislation in which assistance was renamed and destigmatized was less a reform than a confirmation of what was already true in practice.

In the United States, by contrast, the assistance and insurance systems remain separate with respect to unemployment. Receipt of unemployment benefits generally precludes receipt of public assistance. The eligibility focus that is placed on female household heads in the United States means that the role of assistance as an unemployment benefit is far more indirect than it is in Britain. The response of public assistance expenditure to unemployment is difficult to measure in America. In Britain, the relationship is pretty clear, as can be seen in Table 4.1.

TABLE 4.1 Unemployment and Supplementary Benefit Claims, 1961–73

Year	% Unemploy-ment	No. of Unemployment Claimants (in 000s)	No. of unemployed SB Claimants (in 000s)	
			With Unemployment Benefit	Without Unemployment Benefit
1961	1·5	209	45	86
1962	2·0	281	89	113
1963	2·5	390	62	123
1964	1·6	220	38	93
1965	1·4	188	34	78
1966	1·4	208	77	102
1967	2·2	361	86	138
1968	2·4	331	73	147
1969	2·4	309	71	157
1970	2·5	327	73	166
1971	3·3	438	129	258
1972	3·7	372	87	305
1973	2·6	211	48	201

Source: Central Statistical Office, *Annual Abstract of Statistics, 1972* (London: HMSO, 1972), and Department of Health and Social Security, *Social Security Statistics, 1974* (London: HMSO, 1975).

Since the eligibility focus in Britain is the householder, the function of assistance (SB) is to ensure that the unemployed claimant receives the social minimum level of benefits which is represented by the SB scale rate (basic benefit level) plus rent. If the Unemployment Benefit pays at least this much, then SB is not involved. If UB falls short of it, then SB makes up the difference. If the unemployed worker is not eligible for UB, then SB carries the entire burden. The latter case would include new entrants into the full-time labor market, including children aged sixteen even if living at home, re-entrants, and persons moving from self-employment to unemployment. Wives are not householders, and are eligible only for UB, and then only if they had opted to pay the full rate of contribution.

The condition for receiving the Supplementary Benefit is availability for work if the claimant is able-bodied and not an unsupported mother. Availability is evidenced, at minimum, by registration at the Employment Service. As a practical matter, the pressure to get a job is applied with differing intensities to different categories of people. For example, middle-aged widows will be exempted if they have no work experience, and registration is only a formality for older men who are among the long-term unemployed.

The role of SB for unemployment illustrates the shift in the respective roles of assistance and insurance in the British social security system. The last moved quite a distance from the Beveridge concept of income maintenance, a concept that was far more conservative than the present system. Of the various conflicting goals that the Beveridge Plan tried to encompass, the goal of a guaranteed social minimum income for all, subject to a work requirement for the able-bodied, overrode all the others. The work test is satisfied by efforts to find work on the labor market, a condition that will be discussed in Chapter 5.

Supplementary Benefits emerged not so much as the ultimate residual benefit but as a substitute for and supplement to National Insurance benefits. The latter are themselves substitutes and supplements to private savings and private transfer payments, including intra-family transfers and loans. Insurance benefits do not directly deter savings and private transfers, since the social insurance notion excludes the use of the means test. Nevertheless, the presence of National Insurance reduces the need for intra-family transfers and thus reinforces the decomposition of the extended family. Similarly, NI reduces the need to save for various contingencies. To a certain extent, the payroll tax that finances NI also reduces people's ability to make private transfer payments within their kinship circle, and it also reduces their ability to accumulate savings.

All this, of course, reflects the Bismarckian proposition that socialization of savings and insurance against certain contingencies is a course of action that advances the general welfare and political stability of the community.

Hardly anyone quarrels with the need for social insurance, although there may be disputes both over its extent and its use – or lack of use – as a device for vertical redistribution of income. However, the coexistence of SB and NI in the roles described above, creates a number of problems :

(1) If NI benefits are to be 'preferable' to SB, they must pay substantially more in money income.

(2) If money benefits from NI, NI/SB, and SB are not substantially different in magnitude, then the utility (satisfaction) from each pound of SB must somehow be less than the utility of a pound of NI if the preferable status of the latter is to be maintained. This implies a function for stigma, harassment, and the other unpleasantries usually associated with public assistance. The function is to affect the behavior of potential claimants, but it will also affect the behavior of those who administer the two systems. The very process of administration of a means-tested benefit will reinforce this attitude among both claimants and administrators.[12]

(3) A reduction in stigma and associated unpleasantness may be desirable both for humane and for political reasons (given the wide role of SB). However, a consequence of such reduction will be the growth of incentives to claimants to avoid the NI system, and to choose SB to the extent that this may be possible at the margin. High contribution rates for NI also provide this incentive. Avoidance can take lawful or unlawful forms.

For example, married women who are employed may pay NI taxes at a lower rate and receive less coverage, i.e. the lower rate does not entitle them to unemployment benefits under NI.[13] Hence, the choice of coverage for a 'rational' married working woman requires her to predict the probability and length of unemployment for herself or her husband, not to mention predicting the stability of her marriage.

To give another example, there may be an advantage to a worker to be 'self-employed', not only for reasons of income tax advantages (including the possibility of greater tax evasion), but also in order to pay a lower National Insurance contribution.[14] If the benefit is going to be pretty much the same – which would be the case in the lower-than-average wage brackets – then it makes sense to choose the cheapest option. In some lines of work, the option of choosing between employed and self-employed labor is available. The most notorious example is the construction trades, where the growing number of 'self-employed' laborers (i.e. they are independent contractors) is called 'lump labor'. Construction is a low-wage trade in Britain. Accordingly, many workers who need to claim unemployment or pension benefits will get the SB rate regardless of their contributions to NI.[15] Payment of the NI contribution at the full rate would be economically irrational for such workers.

Family Income Supplement and Supplementary Benefits
The two types of payments, FIS and SB, are mutually exclusive. Accordingly, one would not expect a direct interaction between the two. However, as is often the case in social welfare programs, the existence of one benefit affects behavior with respect to the other.

FIS was legislated in 1971 as a form of wage supplementation for low-paid working families with at least one child. There is a 'prescribed amount' of income for each family by the number of children. Income consists of all earnings, except those of children, plus family allowances. The prescribed amount corresponds roughly to a poverty line. In 1975, families with incomes below the prescribed amount were entitled to a supplement of half the amount by which family income fell below the prescribed amount, up to a maximum of £5·50 per week for families with one to two children, and £7 per week where there were three or more minor children.

The benefit, as described above, gives the appearance of a special negative tax system with a negative tax rate of 50 per cent. An important reason for the enactment of negative tax systems is to enhance the claimants' incentives to seek work in the labor market, that is, to make earned income financially preferable to welfare income.[16] This was the prime motivation of the Family Assistance Plan legislation in the United States. The negative tax aspects of FAP were supposed to turn welfare into 'workfare' by raising the incomes of the working poor (in families) relative to the incomes of families subsisting entirely on welfare. This was to solve the problem of the 'welfare mess'.

Like a number of other American observers, I had originally viewed FIS as having a work incentive purpose. My British contacts, however,[17] found this attitude puzzling. The principal purpose of the legislation, I was told, was to help families who were in poverty despite the fact that the head of the family engaged in full-time work. FIS was an alternative to a sharp increase in the size of Family Allowances and the extension of FAM to families with one child. Indeed, the target population was poor children. Where such children had non-working parents, SB brought them up to the poverty line. But FAM, paying 90 pence per week for the second child and £1 for each subsequent child, came nowhere near filling the poverty gap.

Expansion of FAM would have involved a substantial transfer cost, which was why it was favored by the British Left and by those who prefer universal benefits for their absence of stigma and administrative discretion. A 1968 increase in FAM had been financed, in part, by 'claw-back' i.e. by adjusting income taxes so as to recapture the benefits from tax-payers whose incomes were great enough to place them into the 'standard rate' bracket (which was then 32 per cent). However, by 1971, a combination of inflation and tax reform had raised large numbers of low-income wage earners above the tax threshold, paying a standard rate of 30 per cent (plus NI contribution), which was also the *lowest* marginal tax rate. But these same low income families were the target for proposed benefits. Accordingly, there was no scope left for the use of 'claw-back' to concentrate the benefits on the target population.[18]

On closer examination it became clear to me that the function of the negative tax in FIS (plus the absolute limit on the size of the benefit) was to concentrate the benefits on the desired target as precisely and economically as possible. As a result, FIS became a program of modest size, with 72,000 claimants by the end of 1974 (down from the previous year's 95,000 because of the increase in unemployment).[19] Furthermore, much of the discussion about work incentives centered around the *disincentive* effect of an implicit marginal tax rate of 50 per cent especially when added to the tax rates implicit in the other benefits available to this population. FIS, by serving as a 'passport' to other benefits, encourages the take-up of additional benefits and therefore implies an implicit tax rate of well *over* 50 per cent for its beneficiaries. This phenomenon is called the poverty trap because the high 'tax' on additional earnings keeps the worker in poverty.[20] Suffice it to say, FIS was not primarily intended to provide work incentives for what was believed to be an otherwise work-shy population. Although the discussions in the House of Commons on the bill paid lip service to the work ethic, work incentive did not seem to be much of a genuine issue.

In British eyes, FIS marked a radical departure from previous welfare policy in that cash benefits became available to working people for the first time since the demise of the Speenhamland system in the early nineteenth century. The Poor Law reform of 1834 had made work and welfare mutually exclusive, except inside the workhouse, and the tradition persisted into the twentieth century. Rather more to-do than necessary was made of this in Britain, considering that the in-kind benefits already available to this population are a substitute for cash and would affect behavior in a manner very similar to cash benefits. However, the relative attractiveness of SB to low-wage workers must have been on the minds of the FIS planners. Strictly speaking, the incentive to move from low-paid work to SB should be blunted by the wage stop, which would keep SB benefits from being greater than wage earnings. Thus, there should be no interaction between FIS and SB, since if the rules of wage stop are enforced, FIS is not really necessary to protect SB from abuse by economically rational but low-paid workers whose benefits on SB would exceed their wages.

Wage stop is not applied to female heads of households, and presumably SB is preferable to low-wage work to this population, even without considering the cost of child care. The advent of FIS has altered this calculation at the margin. For example, an unsupported mother with two children, aged six and nine, would receive £14·20 plus rent from SB. If she worked at least thirty hours per week and earned, say, £18·00, she would receive 90 pence from FAM and £3·50 from FIS. Thus, she was better off at work to the extent that her rent and work expenses, including payroll taxes, were less than £8·20 per week.[21]

It is therefore not surprising that some unsupported mothers have taken advantage of FIS. Unfortunately, it is not possible here to estimate the extent to which this represents a shift from SB to the labor market. Nevertheless, it is noteworthy that the proportion of FIS claimants who are women has risen steadily from 38 per cent of the case-load in 1972 to 45 per cent in 1973 and 51 per cent in 1974.[22] An analysis of these families by number of children, average benefit, and average earnings is found in Table 4.2. As would be expected, the largest proportion (65 per cent) consists of one child families, since earnings ability relative to the cost of child care falls off sharply after the first child. The average weekly wage for this category was £15.74, which is low by British standards, especially considering the

TABLE 4.2 Mothers with Dependent Children Receiving Family Income Supplement, December 1973

	No. (000s)	%	Average Weekly Benefit	Average Weekly Wage
All families	43	100	2·88	17·10[a]
1 child	28	65	2·77	15·74
2 children	10	23	2·76	17·56
3 or more children	6	12	3·24	19·83

[a] Weighted average.

Source: Computed from data in *Hansard* (Feb 10, 1975) pp. 47–8. Average weekly wages can be estimated by applying the following formula: wage = prescribed income − FAM − $\frac{1}{2}$ of benefit. This assumes that families have no resources except for their wages and FAM. The estimated wage for families with three or more children is computed from a weighted average that assumes the following family size distribution: three children − 68·4 per cent; four children − 20·2 per cent; five children − 7·2 per cent; six children − 4·2 per cent; no significant number with seven or more. This is the distribution for October 1972, for which I was able to receive unpublished data from the Department of Health and Social Security.

fact that it represents at least 30 hours of work. For families with two children, the average wage estimate is £17·56. Note that it takes a higher wage to bring the larger families into the labor market, a factor that points to the role that FIS plays as a labor market incentive.

Much of the controversy over FIS in Britain has hinged on the relatively low rate of take-up. The controversy flared in 1973 when it was estimated that only 60 per cent of the target population claimed the benefit.[23] This raises some wonderment about a program that has trouble giving away money. To the American reader, however, the disproportionate and rising use of FIS by unsupported mothers suggests that there is scope for a wage supplement in aid of single mothers who prefer to work. On the American scene, this is done by the provision of AFDC that enable the recipient to keep 33 per cent of earnings about $30 per month, with disregard for work-related expenses. However, there is an important difference between the two programs that must be noted : the British program is more universal; application can be made by filing a form at the nearest post office, and eligibility is established by proof of employment, earnings, and family status. The American program focuses on the woman who is *unemployed* at the time of application, and thus discriminates against the woman who expresses her desire and ability to work simply by working.

Family Income Supplement interacts with Supplementary Benefits in yet another manner, and that is in connection with wage stop. It will be recalled that the purpose of wage stop is to limit benefits under SB to the claimant's wage alternatives where the latter are smaller than the scale rate (i.e. basic rate). In computing the alternative income available to the claimant on the labor market, his or her FIS entitlement is taken into account and treated as if it were wages. The result has been to raise the benefits of claimants subject to wage stop and to eliminate the wage stop altogether for much of the previously wage-stopped population.

Redundancy Benefits

Redundancy Benefits (RB) are paid as a lump sum to workers who are severed from employment for economic reasons. They apparently combine the concept that workers have a property right in jobs with the function of aiding workers during the transition toward other jobs or toward retirement. The latter function is also performed by National Insurance and Supplementary Benefits for unemployed workers, so that this benefit joins the array of benefits available to certain of the unemployed. There is no direct interaction with NI, in that both benefits are of the social insurance type and are additive. Being unemployed is not a condition for receiving RB, since

C

the award will be made regardless of whether the claimant has another job lined up, or, for that matter, wishes to withdraw from the labor force. There may be an indirect interaction, in that RB may enable workers to prolong their job search, remain unemployed longer and therefore draw more in Unemployment Benefits from NI.

The relationship of RB to SB is similar except that Redundancy Benefits are partially a substitute for SB. This is because RB is treated as part of the family resources in calculating eligibility and the level of benefits. Under the British system, the presence of assets does not disqualify claimants from receiving SB. Capital below the value of £325 is disregarded entirely. Above that amount, weekly benefits are reduced by 5 pence weekly for every £25 up to £800, where the implicit tax rises to $12\frac{1}{2}$ pence per £25. Furthermore, the value of an owner-occupied house is disregarded.[24] Since most RB payments are below £325 (the average is £200) no substitution takes place in these cases. As with NI, any interaction is indirect in that it may prolong the claimant's willingness to remain unemployed.

Training Allowances

The British manpower training program, known as the Training Opportunities Scheme (TOPS) provides cash allowances for workers who are enrolled in the training program. The program itself is described in Chapter 6. It is useful at this point, however, to look at the level of allowances in TOPS as compared to SB and NI. Although training allowances are not commonly thought to be a form of social security, they serve an income maintenance function for persons who might otherwise be unemployed. Indeed, some unemployed persons who might have the opportunity to enroll in TOPS might have to consider the opportunity costs involved, since training allowances are not uniformly higher than SB, which might be an available alternative.

To the extent that training allowances and SB are mutually exclusive, they do not interact directly. The same is true of training allowances and unemployment benefits under NI. As with other alternatives, the presence of one may affect behavior with respect to the other. The incentive to 'choose' on or the other is limited, of course, by administration of the relevant rules governing eligibility and by the limited number of places available in the training program.

It is instructive to examine the benefit levels of the three programs, and this is done in Table 4.3 The benefits under training allowances and NI include Family Allowances where two or more children are involved, so as to facilitate comparison with SB. Earnings-related benefits have been excluded because persons whose unemployment benefit is primarily SB will have exhausted their eligibility for such benefits. The reader is reminded, however, that the training allowances and NI benefits in Table 4.3 understate the actual benefits for workers who in recent previous employment were earning over £9 per week.

SB is cited at the scale rate, i.e. without rent. Since the benefit varies both with family size and age of children, I have simplified the table by assuming that all children are either under five years old or, at the other extreme, between the ages of thirteen and fifteen.[25] This establishes the range of the scale rate.

The columns headed 'Equalizing Rent Factor' show the difference between the Training Allowance and the SB scale rate. Thus, the cash benefit under the Training Allowance is equal to or greater than SB when the rent (or housing cost) is equal to or less than the equalizing rent factor. It is assumed that all families collect the relevant rent rebates and allowances.

Training Allowances are greater than NI unemployment benefits – even for women (women are entitled to lower Training Allowances than men). Making Training Allowances greater than NI benefits was a deliberate policy to encourage unemployed persons to take up training. A spokesman for the Department of Employment pointed out to me that Training Allowances were also greater than the SB scale rate, and said that this too was a deliberate policy to encourage training. However, the comparison between the latter two types of benefits is not so simple, because of the roles played by age of children and level of rent.[26]

Training Allowances tend to be more generous than SB for single persons and for very small families who were not likely, in 1972, to be paying £4 to £5 per week in housing costs – at least, outside of London. Presumably, this would include unsupported mothers. The younger the children, the greater the relative advantage of Training Allowance over SB, since the SB scale rate varies with the age of the children.

The above implies that Training Allowances (relative to SB) favor younger workers to the extent that workers with young children are likely to be younger than those with older children. The age distribution of single persons and couples without children is bimodal. However, since many of the workers with fully grown children are likely to be too old to be candidates for training,[27] the inclusion of single persons and households with two adults does not alter the conclusion that Training Allowances are biased toward younger workers. The relative advantage is extremely great where one adult can train while the other works. A working spouse does not disqualify the family from Training Allowances, but would disqualify it from SB.

TABLE 4.3 Relation of Training Allowance to National Insurance and Supplementary Benefits, for Comparable Cases, 1974

Family size and Composition	TA + FAM[a,b]	NI + FAM[a,b]	SB Scale Rate			Equalizing Rent Factor			Average Rent[c,d]
			None	Children Young	Older	None	Children Young	Older	
	£ p	£ p	£ p	£ p	£ p	£ p	£ p	£ p	£ p
Man, no dependents	13·60	8·60	8·40			5·20			2·17[c]
Man and wife	17·90	13·90	13·65			4·25			2·40[e]
Man, wife, 1 child	20·10	16·60		16·05	18·00		4·05	2·10	3·41[e]
Man, wife, 2 children	22·80	19·30		18·45	22·35		4·35	·45	3·90[d]
Man, wife, 3 children	25·50	22·00		20·85	26·70		4·65	−1·20	4·40[d]
Woman, no dependents	13·60	8·60	8·40						2·17[d]
Woman, 1 child	15·80	11·30		10·80	12·75		5·00	3·05	3·41[d]
Woman, 2 children	18·50	14·00		13·20	17·10		5·30	1·40	3·90[d]

[a] Plus earnings-related benefit, where applicable. Training Allowances cited here are for living at home. Trainees also receive lunch, car-fare (if the Centre is more than two miles from home), and credit for NI contributions. Rates are for adults over twenty years old. Rates for women are at the scale for single women.
[b] FAM is included in order to establish comparability with SB.
[c] Average rents are taken from Department of Health and Social Security, *Annual Report, 1973*, p. 80.
[d] Crude estimate.

Sources: Training Services Agency, *Training Allowances/Weekly Rates*, TSAL 9 (July 1974); Department of Health and Social Security, *Benefit Rates from July 1974*, NI 196/74 (June 1974); Department of Health and Social Security, *Supplementary Pensions and Allowances*, SB.1 (July 1974).

The effect of favoring younger households may be desirable from a cost–benefit point of view. Benefits in cost–benefit analysis are the present value of the future stream of earnings increments, and it is the nature of the formula to assign greater values to younger workers. However, if a policy goal is greater employability for the long-term unemployed, including workers suffering from technological unemployment in mid-career, then the relative incentives of Training Allowances and SB are behaving perversely.[28]

A similar perverse effect is occasioned by the variation that rent (and other housing costs) induces in the total benefit level of SB, and in the relative advantages of Training Allowances to SB. Rents are highest in urban centers, and especially high in the London region. But employment opportunities are greatest in such places, especially in the high-rent London area and its conurbations. Thus, the payoff to training is greatest here, but the short-run incentive is weakest, and the signal sent by the two benefits is confusing.

Arguably, a comparison of SB and Training Allowances is misleading in that training involves long-term expectations. Thus, even though SB benefits may exceed Training Allowances for any given family, the difference constitutes part of the family's investment in the trainee's stock of human capital. There is nothing unusual about forgoing present consumption for the future, and it is certainly done by trainees who enroll directly from other jobs or who have wage alternatives that exceed the Training Allowance. In 1971, some 40 per cent of applicants to Government Training Centres were employed at the time of application,[29] and these took a reduction in income in order to engage in training. However, unemployed parents in their middle years who have school-aged children, have less of an economic margin for investment than younger couples, especially if their housing costs are high.[30]

The direction of financial incentives appears to be consonant with other relevant policies, although the consonance may be unintentional. At the operative level, training programs tend to discriminate against older persons and the long-term unemployed. Older persons are said to have more problems, to be harder to work with, and to require more help. Managers of training facilities measure their success by graduates and placements, so that the older men present greater risk of failure not only to themselves but to the trainers' success indicia.

Consonance also exists with FIS, which has made job-holding relatively more advantageous for unsupported mothers. The relative benefits of Training Allowances to SB for a woman with one child lie in the same direction. Data are not available on the extent to which such women are in training, or the training opportunities that exist for them. However, the expansion of TOPS includes an expansion of training opportunities for women, and this will incidentally pick up some of the mothers.

When income maintenance programs are viewed as a set, their benefits are seen to constitute a structure of incentives and disincentives that affect labor market behavior. This structure is not necessarily consonant with the set of explicit goals that are intended by the various programs. As American readers know, the less generous American structure suffers from a similar kind of program irrationality stemming from the interaction of apparently separate programs.

WORK DISINCENTIVES AND POVERTY TRAP

The existence of income maintenance programs with benefit rates that are high relative to earnings opportunities creates an obvious problem that has long been recognized. The claimant whose wage opportunity is no greater – or not much greater – than his benefits does not have a powerful incentive to seek work. Sanctions and controls are commonly found in such situations to cajole or compel labor market behavior. Alternatively, the claimant is said to be trapped in poverty, since his efforts to improve his economic situation by working are relatively fruitless.

One approach to solving this problem has been to diminish benefits less rapidly than the increment in earned income. Income-conditioned benefits of this sort employ the negative tax principle, and have the characteristic of concentrating benefits on a specified target group. The supposed advantage – that beneficiaries are induced to work since they keep some of the gains – has come under dispute in recent years, both in Britain and in the United States. This is because the rate of benefit loss can be quite high, especially in situations where multiple benefits are taken up by the claimant.

In the United States, public assistance payments such as AFDC may be drawn by working women, along with Medicaid benefits, food stamps, and housing allowances. Henry Aaron has shown that a family of four receiving these benefits can face implicit marginal tax rates of 75 per cent to 80 per cent, with a serious notch (i.e. rate well above 100 per cent) at the point where the major benefits are lost.[31] A more detailed study of the Joint Economic Committee showed a bewildering variety of benefit – loss rates in American income security programs.[32] Both studies, and others like them, stress the incentive effect of high implicit marginal tax rates. The notion of poverty trap, which is the reverse of the coin, is relatively alien to American thinking.

In Britain, A. R. Prest drew attention to the high tax rates of multiple benefits in his influential *Social Benefits and Tax Rates,* published in 1970.[33] Prest was concerned with work incentives. The following year, David Piachaud raised the issue from the other point of view : the high rates trap persons into poverty.[34] Concern with work incentives of high tax rates was one of the reasons for the Conservative government's proposal for a tax credit system.[35] This was a negative tax scheme designed to rationalize various existing benefits (except for SB) into a more coherent cash system, and to integrate the benefits with the positive income tax in order to minimize overlaps. The principal benefits to be replaced were to have been Family Income Supplement and Family Allowances. An important argument for the proposal was that it would reduce the high marginal tax rates paid by low-income families.[36]

Actually, economic theory is not very helpful in predicting the impact of high marginal tax rates on labor market behavior. The income effect of high tax rates is to reduce a person's ability to afford leisure time. The substitution effect, on the other hand, serves to reduce the opportunity cost of leisure time, making it relatively more desirable. Although it is commonly believed that the substitution effect is the dominant one on net balance, there is remarkably little empirical evidence on the subject, especially for rates below 100 per cent.[37]

The impact of high marginal tax rates is somewhat blunted in Britain by two administrative practices. The first is the device of awarding certain benefits for a fixed period of time. The second consists of 'uprating', annually adjusting benefit levels to reflect increases in consumer prices. For example, Family Income Supplement is awarded for one year at a time, and brings with it eligibility for free school lunches, rent and rate rebates,[38] and a variety of benefits such as waivers of the fees for eye glasses, prescription drugs, and dental care. The benefit levels are periodically changed as prices rise.

The actual marginal tax rate to which a family is subject depends on the number benefits which its uses. Prest used twelve available benefits in his analysis, Bradshaw and Wakeman used seven, while Fiegehen and Lansley confined themselves to four benefits that can be received on a regular basis in distinction to those that are claimed only when the need arises.[39] Assuming that work behavior is affected, the impact will vary not only with the family's perception of its marginal tax rate, but also with its assessment of the value of benefits in kind, and with the timing of its application for benefits and their renewals. Although few people know what their marginal tax rates are, I suspect than even fewer are unaware when additional work effort brings little or no reward.

The fixed-period awards serve to protect short-term variations in earnings that fall within the period of the award. This includes such earnings as occasional overtime, shift work, and second job holdings, as well as temporary or seasonal job holdings by a secondary earner in the family. The additional earnings from such work are subject only to the National Insurance tax and to income tax if the income tax threshold is crossed.

Earnings variations of the type described above are not uncommon among chronically low-wage workers. Little hard evidence is available, but some support for the hypothesis comes from a survey of three low wage industries in Britain conducted at the beginning of 1971 (i.e. before the introduction of FIS with its 50 per cent marginal tax rate). The survey found that 36 per cent of full-time males in the low-pay group were working overtime during the survey week, most of them for additional gross sums of £1 to £4; 23 per cent reported frequent opportunity to work overtime.[40]

The fixed period of benefits also gives some temporary protection, lasting from a month to a year, to low-wage families who manage to increase their earnings on a more permanent basis. Some of these are families whose normally high earnings are temporarily depressed by short-time work or the unemployment of one earner in a two-earner family, and who can pass through the poverty trap on the resumption of their normal earning power. Some others, whose increased earnings only bring them into the range of high marginal tax rates, derive protection from uprating. Here, the periodic rise in benefits and in the level of 'prescribed income' below which benefits are paid protects the nominal value of net family income for earners whose gross incomes rise in average earnings.[41]

The tentative conclusion from the available evidence is that on the whole, income-tested benefits by themselves may not present as severe a problem of work disincentive or poverty trap as has been commonly supposed. They present other problems, of course, including serious inequities between persons whose circumstances are similar in all respects except for the timing of their grants, and they may offer an incentive to low-pay workers to 'bunch' their earnings in order to maximize their grants. There is no evidence on this last phenomenon in Britain. However, we know that American workers, confronted by an income-tested unemployment benefit in Wisconsin that offered a similar opportunity, maneuvered their earnings in order to maximize their income.[42] It is possible that British workers may also be learning how to do this.

The behavior of potential claimants is affected not only by incentives and disincentives, but also by sanctions. And it is to these that we must now turn.

5 Britain: The Control Procedures

The devices that encourage or compel labor market activity by public assistance claimants may be divided into pushes and pulls. Pushes, in general, are rules and practices that make the claimant worse off by not working. Worse off, however, includes not only practices that punish economically, but also those that include other pressures. Pulls, on the other hand, are policies that make the claimant economically better off if he enters the labor market. Although the latter have become more important in recent years, especially since the development of negative income tax ideas, pushes remain an important aspect of public assistance labor market policy. Indeed, when benefits are high relative to the claimants' realistic alternatives in the labor market, then the reliance on pushes will be great, since economic incentives become costly in terms of public funds.

Benefits that encourage work and training are Family Income Supplements (which were previously discussed) and the Training Opportunities Scheme with its training allowances (which will be covered in more detail in Chaper 6). In the pages below we shall examine the pushes : control procedures that include the four-week rule, periodic review of claims, direction to attend a Re-establishment Centre, and prosecution for failure to maintain oneself or dependents. Additionally, the wage stop will be discussed although, strictly speaking, it is more of a pull than a push. Nevertheless, it can function in a punitive fashion like some of the other controls.

THE FOUR-WEEK RULE
In areas where jobs for unskilled men are generally available (areas so designated by the Department of Employment), a claimant who is unskilled, single, and under forty-five years of age must reapply for Supplementary Benefits at the end of four weeks. The period may

be shorter if seasonal work is available. The process of reapplication involves a review of the applicant's job search activities, and his reasons for not obtaining work. The claimant also reports to the Labor Exchange which tries to place him, and which makes the actual SB payment. The operation of the control is summarized in Table 5.1

TABLE 5.1 Operation of the Four-Week Rule, 1971–3

	1971	1972	1973
Unemployment rate (%)	3·3	3·7	2·6
Total SB claims from unemployed persons	387,000	392,000	249,000
Number of four-week awards	62,250	14,500	17,403
as % of all awards	16·1	3·7	7·0
Number of renewal applications	6,479	1,900	1,138
as % of four-week awards	10·4	13·1	6·5
Renewals refused	1,663	323	351
as % of renewal applications	25·7	17	30·8

Source: Department of Health and Social Security, *Annual Reports, 1971, 1972,* and *1973.*

A number of things emerge from Table 5.1. One is that the actual numbers involved are relatively small in relation to total claims. In 1971, four-week awards constituted 16 per cent of all awards, and in 1972 they declined to 3·7 per cent of all awards. Evidently, some policy change occurred, but the rule is also sensitive to aggregate unemployment conditions. What is equally of interest is the relatively small number of renewal applications at the end of four weeks. In 1971 these were 10·4 per cent of all four-week awards; they had risen to 13·1 per cent by 1972, declining to 6·5 per cent in the low unemployment year of 1973. This implies that the rule may be successful as a control mechanism, in that it either encourages claimants to engage in active job search because they know that they will be subjected to scrutiny at the end of four weeks, or that it discourages reapplications from persons who might otherwise be eligible.

However, there may be other explanations for the low rate of reapplication. Even during a period of high unemployment, the labor market for unskilled workers has job vacancies resulting from turnover, so that one would expect a certain number of men to have found jobs by the end of the period. Another contributing factor might be the delay involved in getting Unemployment Benefits; these, in many cases, are high enough to disqualify claimants from SB once payment on them begins. In terms of the ratio of benefits to wage alternatives, unskilled single men do not have a powerful incentive to engage in scrounging, beyond resting up a bit between jobs. The 1974 scale rate for a single householder was £8·40 weekly, plus addition for net rent; even if rent is calculated generously at £5 (the Commission can disallow 'unreasonably high' rents), the total is still well below what the labor market will bring. For persons living with their parents the addition for rent is 90 pence. If such claimants are young, say nineteen, the £9·30 might be enough for a while as pocket money, and the incentive for staying on SB might be greater than is indicated by the ratio of benefits to wages. The fact of the matter is that no one knows.

Whether or not the four-week rule is a functionally operative control, either directly or through deterrence, it does serve the politically important function of helping to satisfy the public that 'something is being done'. This, at least, was the view given to me by one civil servant, whose general outlook did not reveal excessive sympathy for claimants.

THE PROCESS OF REVIEW

Another example of controls which appear to be a mix of help, hassle, and threat are the reviews conducted both by local office Unemployment Review Officers or staff performing this function, and by the regional UROs. Claimants whose cases are reviewed are called in for interviews. As a general proposition, the local officers tend to concentrate on short-term claims, and the regional UROs put emphasis on longer-term claims and on claims that are made with excessive frequency.

It is believed in Britain that the review process succeeds in reducing the SB case-load. Existing data appear to bear this out, although the data are too sparse to provide a firm basis for this conclusion. In 1972, 73,000 persons were called for special interviews by their local office, and 40,000 'went off the books' before or shortly after the interview. Regional UROs called 40,000 persons, of whom 19,000 went off the books before or shortly after.[1] Some of this is normal turnover, and some undoubtedly involves 'turning the pile', since data do not exist to show how many of the men reappear on the rolls.

A more detailed breakdown was not available for 1972. However, unpublished statistics for one month in 1970 show that 15·5 per cent of claimants called for interview went off the 'E load' (i.e. list of employable claimants) before the date of the interview, and another 24·2 per cent went off shortly after one or two interviews. About 10 per cent of those actually interviewed had their allowances limited or withdrawn. There was considerable variation from region to region in this behavior. The relative number of cases in which allowances were limited or withdrawn correlates roughly with the level of employment opportunities.[2]

The interview process is supposed to be helpful to the claimant and the Supplementary Benefit Commission puts great stress on this. At the same time, the Unemployment Review Officers, and others exercising a similar function, view as one of their tasks the ridding of the rolls of scroungers. Indeed, this view is pervasive enough so that individual staff members may judge the success of their efforts by the number of people who leave the 'E load'. Local office staff are said to have strong views on the subject, and these views may be strengthened where staff are paying out benefits to unemployed workers that are greater than their own salaries.

According to the Commission itself :

> The Unemployment Review Officer is operating in an area where society's attitudes to the Commission's functions are ambivalent. On the one hand, the Commission are urged to deal firmly with 'scroungers and layabouts' content to 'sponge upon the State' : on the other it is accused of 'chivvying' and labeling as 'work shy' those who are unable to get work, perhaps when unemployment is rising.[3]

Regional Unemployment Review Officers now take a two-week course at the School of Social Work at the University of Leicester, and there is a general trend toward moving UROs along a road toward social work.[4]

RE-ESTABLISHMENT

The next level of severity in the control procedures is the suggestion – or requirement – that the claimant attend a Re-establishment Centre. More will be said of these in the chapter that follows since they have an interesting but unused potential for retraining. The Centres, which are operated by DHSS under Section 34 of the 1966 Act, are the lineal descendants of the workhouse. Long-term unemployed men – but never women – may be referred to them for the purpose of helping them 'back into the habit and routine of a normal working life, for which they have become unfitted'.[5] There is something quaint about the wording of this text; alternatively, it conjures up visions of a twenty-first-century behavior modification camp where layabouts are reprogrammed into hard-working proles. In fact, as we shall see in another context, the Centres are an almost forgotten activity. They deal, in all, with about 2000 men per year.[6] Although only about 2 per cent of the men are there under the explicit threat that their allowances would otherwise be reduced, it is widely believed that many of those who attend on a voluntary basis do so for essentially the same reason. The Centres should not be confused with Reception Centres, which are operated by DHSS for homeless men. The confusion is often made in Britain, even by officials of the Supplementary Benefits Commission who were interviewed by the writer; the confusion becomes understandable when one learns that a number of Re-establishment Centres are run jointly with Reception Centres.

With respect to the control procedures discussed so far, the underlying sanction has been reduction or suspension of the Supplementary Allowance. It should further be noted that most of the persons in question were also subjected to administrative pressure to find a job through their contact with the Department of Employment's Labour Exchanges. Unemployed SB claimants must register for work (unless they fall into the exempt categories of unsupported mothers, late-middled-aged widows, etc.) along with claimants for Unemployment Benefits under National Insurance Thus, refusal to take a suitable job and similar malingering behavior comes under the scrutiny of the staff of the Employment Exchange. For most claimants, it also means queuing up weekly, a process which may keep them from accepting their unemployed status as permanent. Legally, the process of reducing or withholding allowances is likely to require some certification by the Employment Exchange that the claimant is shirking possible work, under circumstances similar to those that would threaten his eligibility for National Insurance Unemployment Benefits. The usual penalty is a reduction of benefit by 40 per cent of the single householder scale, for a maximum of six weeks. This amounts to £3·36 per week, or about 14 per cent of the benefit that a married householder with two children, paying £5 rent, would receive. Benefits can be refused under some circumstances, but only for the individual, and not for his dependents (except a 'fit' wife without children).

FAILURE TO MAINTAIN

The ultimate sanction is prosecution for 'persistent failure or neglect to maintain himself or any other person he is liable to maintain'. The number of men who are actually prosecuted is a miniscule percentage of the case-load of long-term unemployed men (never women), and it has declined in recent years. In 1971, eighty-five men were considered for prosecution, of whom sixty-four were actually prosecuted; only one man was acquitted (case dismissed) and only eleven men actually served jail sentences.[7] The number prosecuted dropped to seventeen during 1972[8] because the Department of Health and Social Security did not have the staff time available to do a proper job. Since the Department's record of convictions is 99 per cent (404 out of 409 in the period 1968–71), it is clear that some care is taken in the preparation of each case.

One is tempted to wonder who the sacrificial victims are, and how they are selected. Olive Stevenson suggests that some of the men who are prosecuted are 'the least adequate of a group who evade work'.[9] In view of the fact that the British system is very oriented toward considering the welfare of the client and his family, and very understanding of personality and family problems, illness, and a long number of 'etceteras', the visitor is inclined to agree that anyone with a minimal amount of wit can escape prosecution. But the logic of the system demands prosecution, since cutting off family benefits is not an available alternative. Presumably, some level of prosecution is needed to maintain the credibility of the threat.

WAGE STOP

In Britain, as in the United States, the wage that an individual worker can command in the labor market is not related to family size. The Family Allowance, Family Income Supplement (for low-wage workers only) and tax relief (similar to exemptions for dependents in the United States) do combine to introduce some variability into net family income in accordance with family size. This variability, however, is nowhere as great as the variability in income from Supplementary Benefits. This is because SB payments are, in theory, based on need, and need is seen as an increasing function of family size and housing costs. In the low-wage sector of the labor market it easily becomes possible that benefits will be greater than the relevent wage opportunity. Wage stop is an administrative device applied to those claimants who are required to register for work. It limits their benefit so that their income while unemployed is not greater than it would be if they were fully employed in their normal occupations. In 1972, some 6·4 per cent of unemployed SB recipients were wage stopped, a number that declined to 4 per cent in 1973.[10]

At first glance, wage stop looks like a version of the old Poor Law concept of less eligibility, under which benefits were always supposed to be lower than any wage that might be available in the labor market. Strictly speaking, less eligibility referred to the lowest existing wage, and thus provided a standing incentive to work, since work always yielded a greater income. In its heyday, it was a cruel device not merely because the lowest existing wage was a very low real wage, indeed, but also because it was commonly applied to persons who might not, by today's standards, be expected to go to work. Much of the bad reputation that it earned in the nineteenth century stems from the latter aspect. Wage stop, however, might be thought of as 'no-more-than-equal' eligibility. It only applies to claimants who are required to register for work, which is to say that it excludes unsupported mothers from its provisions.

The Supplementary Benefits Commission insists that wage stop is not intended to be an incentive to get work. The basis for wage stop is equity, the reasoning being that it would be 'unfair to the man who was working but whose income was less than the supplementary benefit level if his counterpart who was unemployed received more in benefits'.[11] If an anomaly is seen, it comes from the situation that either some wages are too low or that some benefits are too high. Since the British interpret their SB scale rates as their poverty line, they view wage stop as 'a harsh reflection of the fact that there are many men in work living on incomes below the Supplementary Benefits standard'.[12]

The issue of incentive is not so easily disposed of. Wage stop may place a man on the point of indifference between work and non-work, leaving to the controls the task of overcoming a natural preference for leisure under those circumstances. But it also reduces a positive disincentive to work, albeit at the ethically uncomfortable cost of asking such claimants to live at levels below those approved by Parliament for others.[13] The difference between an incentive and a non-disincentive is surely one of degree rather than kind. The total sort of neutrality that the Commission imagines wage stop to have could be achievable only by extraordinarily brilliant administration, which this measure certainly does not enjoy. This is because there is considerable judgment involved in estimating what a man's net earnings (after taxes, expenses, etc.) might be if he were regularly employed, especially in an economy where earnings variations introduced by overtime are common. Estimation difficulties are especially great for persons who are likely to fall afoul of the wage stop, that is, men with a history of relatively low-paid unskilled work and long spells of unemployment.

As a result of the amount of discretion involved in the application of wage stop, some benefits have undoubtedly been stopped down too low, while others have been assessed at levels too high with respect to the policy. As a result, wage stop has functioned as an incentive mechanism with regard to persons in the former category. Perhaps this was not always unintentional on the part of the civil servants who make the assessment; people who have to exercise judgment are human and do not always leave their policy ideas at home. But the reverse is also true; wage stop has undoubtedly also been applied too lightly, or not at all, in many cases where official policy would have required it. Few people in the British civil service genuinely enjoy playing Scrooge.

In order to reduce the amount of discretion in the system, the

Supplementary Benefits Commission adopted some reforms in 1967. It accepts, as a measure of earnings opportunities, the collectively bargained wage set by the National Joint Council for Local Authorities for manual workers employed by local governments. This is used where no obviously proper wage can be established, and serves as a minimum.[14] Since it tends to be on the high side of the low end of the labor market, it weakens the incentive (or non-disincentive) feature of wage stop. Generally speaking, it favors people in the lower-paid northern regions, as against the higher-wage southern labor market. As was seen in Chapter 3, the Family Income Supplement has also reduced the impact of wage stop. An unintentional incentive feature remains where inflation proceeds faster than either adjustments in scale rates or the administrative reviews of other benefits to which claimants are entitled.

It is time now to leave the depressing world of benefit administration, and turn to the more cheerful topic of helping people to improve their earning powers. In the chapter that follows, an assessment will be made of British manpower policies, both for the mainstream of the working population and for the hard to employ.

6 British Manpower Policy

In the preceding chapters, I have tried to show that any income maintenance policy subsumes a labor market policy – or set of policies – for its target population. The policy set can be inferred from benefit levels, rules of eligibility, and administration. As is frequently the case, inferred policies may differ from official or stated goals. The target population that we have been considering here consists of persons who are 'fit', i.e. potentially employable. Broadly speaking, such persons are also the potential subjects of a nation's manpower policy. Income maintenance and manpower policies overlap, in that both deal with the labor market performance of their constituents. In the pages that follow, we shall look at the integration – or lack of integration – of the two policies in Britain. First, however, it will be useful to describe the background to British manpower policy and the major programs that are of specific relevance to this study.

The origins of British manpower policy lie in the relatively poor performance of the British economy in the late 1950s and early 1960s, at a time when many other western European nations (including non-members of the EEC) began their remarkable period of economic growth. In Britain, then as now, any boom that might have developed had to be aborted quickly because of its rapid translation into inflation and balance of payments problems. The latter were probably aggravated by the role of sterling as a reserve currency and a concomitant need to 'defend' the pound, but the fundamental problem was a structural one. Accordingly, the emergence of an active manpower policy in Britain was in response to a perceived need for a more efficient utilization of human resources. The Industrial Training Act that was enacted in 1964 was part of a policy set that included measures (1) to shift employment from service industries to manufacturing (Selective Employment Tax), (2) to encourage the movement of firms from the crowded south-eastern region into less developed areas by the use of investment grants, tax allowances, employment premiums and similar devices, and (3) to encourage, but only minimally, the flow of labor from areas of surplus to areas of shortage (Resettlement and Employment Transfer Schemes). The last was a very half-hearted policy, and bears little discussion.[1] Since some of these programs were expected to 'shake-out' the labor market, a form of severance pay (Redundancy Benefit) was legislated, both to ease the economic impact on disemployed workers and to reduce the resistance of unions to the disemployment of less productive labor.

The Industrial Training Act of 1964 was designed to promote the development of formal training programs by employers on an industry basis. Thirty Industrial Training Boards (ITBs) were created, with representatives from management, unions, educational establishments, and government. The ITBs were required to plan the establishment of training facilities in order to meet their industry's assessed manpower needs. Each industry could develop its own methods, including formalized on-the-job training, employer-sponsored training programs, industry training centers, courses at educational institutions, and so forth. ITBs were also empowered to levy a tax on their members, and to use the funds to make grants in support of the training programs. The entire system was somewhat loosely coordinated by a Central Training Council in the Ministry of Labour (later called the Department of Employment). In addition to the funds generated by the levies, the government made grants and loans to the ITBs. This training establishment was largely preserved in 1973 legislation that reorganized the employment and training services, although some changes in financing were made to relieve the cost burden on employers.

Gary Hansen has noted that the Industrial Training Act was designed primarily to provide skill training for those who leave school, and only secondarily to retrain workers who have been made redundant. In both instances, the intent was to relieve skill shortages rather than to cope with unemployment.[2] From their inception, the Boards resisted attempts to extend their responsibilities beyond their own industries and beyond any policy goal except training to increase productivity for their industry. The obligation to maintain full employment at the macroeconomic level rested with government, and so did the obligation to provide for the social welfare of the unemployed. It was felt that an industry might try to retrain its own redundant workers for its own redevelopment, but that was, and still is, the furthest extent of the role of the ITBs with respect to the unemployed.

One usually associates Britain's active manpower policy with the Industrial Training Act that created the ITBs. As can be seen, however, the ITBs are not a vehicle for the retraining of the longer-term unemployed workers whom the officials of the Supplementary Benefits Commission and the Employment Service are trying to return to the labor market. Quite the contrary: workers displaced from their employment are obliged to fall out of the industry-based stream of training; they become, as Santos Mukerjee has put it, 'hard luck cases' for whom other forms of retraining are not easily available.[3] Thus, certain government-sponsored programs to increase industrial productivity can generate some long-term and permanent unemployment among workers, and Supplementary Benefit payments become their means of support after National Insurance benefits have been exhausted. Part or all of the Redundancy Benefits may be retained, as explained in a previous chapter, as a sort of consolation prize.[4]

Government Training Centres

The British government has operated some vocational training facilities since 1917, when 'instructional factories' were established to train disabled war veterans. The Government Training Centres (GTCs) survived as a minor sort of operation to help the unemployed after 1925. With the exception of World War II and the immediate post-war period, the GTCs role was social rather than economic, with a target population of ex-servicemen, unemployed, and disabled workers. In this respect, GTCs resembled American manpower programs, in that they dealt with an unemployment problem. By 1962 there were only thirteen GTCs in operation, with fewer than 2500 training slots.

In 1963, the GTCs became part of Britain's active manpower policy. In the following years, the number of Centres rose to fifty-two, with 11,000 training slots.[5] In 1973, plans were made to open another seventeen GTCs and to bring the total number of training slots up to 30,000.[6] The expansion is part of the new Training Opportunities Scheme (TOPS),[7] which encompasses expanded adult vocational education at Colleges of Further Education, as well as the use of spare training capacity in employers' establishments.

The training expansion that occurred after 1963 brought with it a shift in policy away from the social goal of helping unemployed workers and toward the economic goal of furthering economic growth by increasing the supply of skilled labor in shortage occupations.[8] This led to an admissions policy at GTCs that favored workers most likely to succeed, i.e. younger workers whose education and experience made them most suitable for training to upgrade skills. In this sense, the GTCs parallelled the ITBs' rejection of a social role. Note that both were part of an effort to increase productivity, an effort that, if successful, would create technological unemployment. Unlike the ITBs, however, the GTCs were available to unemployed workers, who always constituted a fair proportion of their clientele.

A survey of GTC trainees conducted in 1968–9 showed that 23·3 per cent were not working before entry, and an unspecified proportion were holding 'fill-in' jobs while waiting to enter.[9] Perhaps more to the point, 29·1 per cent of all trainees indicated that leaving their usual or last job was not entirely their own choice. This group tended to be older (over forty-three) than those who left under their own volition.[10]

More recent information on the use of GTCs by unemployed workers will be forthcoming from a survey of GTC trainees that was carried out by Queen Mary College in 1972, at a time when unemployment was higher than in 1968–9. Unpublished data from the study show that 55 per cent of the trainees in the sample were unemployed at the time of the application to a GTC. Twenty-one per cent had no regular employment six to twelve months before entry, which means that the earnings-related portion of their NI benefits had been used up. Of the trainees who had regular work six to twelve months before entry into the GTC, the reasons for leaving were :

	%
Made Redundant	28·2
Fearing Redundancy	4·8
Discharged from Armed Forces	20·6
Ill Health	3·3
To Take Training	35·3
Other	20·6
No answer	1·8
TOTAL	100

The QMC Survey only included persons *accepted* for training, and no data are available in the proportion of applicants who were unemployed or expecting unemployment. However, some insight into the role played by government training in the expectations of unemployed men can be gained from the University of Oxford survey of unemployed men conducted in Coventry, Hammersmith, and Newcastle in October 1971.[11] The published data show that a substantial number of men did not even know of the existence of government training : the percentages were 43·8 in Coventry, 28·0 in Hammersmith, and 23·9 in Newcastle. Unpublished data from the survey that were made available to me indicate that the proportions of the sample who had ever applied for government training (both GTCs and IRUs) were 8·9 per cent and 7·3 per cent in Coventry and Hammersmith, respectively, and 22 per cent in Newcastle. The last is in a depressed area of long standing, which may help to explain the relatively high number. Not all applicants were rejected, of course : some had withdrawn their applications and others were still awaiting word. The majority of those who applied and were rejected were unskilled workers. Age also played a role in the rejections.[12]

The Training Opportunities Scheme (TOPS)

The Government Training Centres are a part of the expanding Training Opportunities Scheme, and can be discussed in this larger context. The basis for TOPS lies in a document called *Training for the Future* which sets out the goals of current British manpower training policy. The primary goals are seen as providing :

(1) training arranged by particular employers to meet their own immediate or foreseeable needs;

(2) training going beyond the obvious needs of particular employers but necessary to meet the foreseeable needs of an an industry;

(3) training given to individuals to meet national economic needs, going beyond the obvious needs of particular industries; and,

(4) training given to individuals to enable them to take new – or better – jobs which they cannot get without first acquiring new skills.

The document stresses the need to integrate training schemes with adult education. Accordingly, TOPS reflects an added emphasis on vocational education in various forms : part-time, full-time, 'sandwich courses', and so forth. In general, *Training for the Future* suggests that the burden of meeting industry needs continues to lie with the Industry Boards and other employer and union programs, whereas training to meet the needs of individuals will be carried out under TOPS.[13]

The new emphasis on the needs of individuals does not, however, detract from the older and larger goal of training for economic growth rather than for social purposes. This is not said in order to fault the scheme but merely to clarify what is being done. The aim of TOPS is to help men and women become fit for better jobs. For this purpose, workers who already hold jobs are the major target group. TOPS is not aimed at persons who have just left school. The training of new entrants into the labor market is held to be the responsibility of employers.

Training is carried out at GTCs and at Technical Colleges. A small but interesting part of the plan is to run short courses in employers' own training establishments where spare places are available.[14]

The planning for TOPS involves setting a national target and breaking this into regional targets on the basis of the supply of places and the demand for training. Estimates of the demand for training are made not only from data on unemployment but also from applications that come from persons currently employed or currently out of the labor market, such as housewives. Selective advertising is used to stimulate the applications and to test the market.

The Employment and Training Act

Training for the Future led to 1973 legislation[15] that created a Manpower Services Commission to coordinate training and placement. The new Commission is a tri-partite body, the intent being to give responsibility for manpower services to representatives of employers, unions, and local government authorities. Presumably, this insulates manpower policy from national politics. The training and placement functions of the Commission were put into two separate agencies : the Training Services Agency (TSA) and the Employment Services Agency (ESA). They are both statutory corporations (i.e. legally independent of the Department of Employment) whose governing boards are appointed by the Commission.

Social Goals v. Economic Goals. There is little doubt that the primary function of manpower policy as carried out by the ITBs and TOPS is economic rather than social. This merged in my discussions with both middle and higher-level officials at the Department of Employment and at visits to training sites. One official who was closely involved in planning the new programs said that American emphasis on training the hard-core unemployed was misdirected, in that assistance for the disadvantaged was a separate problem from training. The implication was that this was a kind of social work to be carried on elsewhere, and not to be confused with the goal of making an economy more efficient. According to this official, TOPS was certainly interested in unemployed workers, but there was no expectation that the program would have any impact on the long-term unemployed.

Discussions with people closer to the operating level of GTCs revealed a similar indisposition to train older or longer-term unemployed workers. It was felt that they were harder to train, more set in their ways, and likelier to have health or personal problems that would interfere with training. The suspicion of being work-shy tended to attach to long-term unemployed men, and GTCs did not want to be the enforcement arm of the Supplementary Benefits Commission. GTCs take pride in their ability to place graduates in employment, and their admissions process tries to skim the cream of the pool of applicants in the relevant catchment area.[16]

Nevertheless, a number of older men manage to enter Government

Training. The Queen Mary College Survey shows that 20 per cent of the sample of 1060 trainees in the survey were over forty years old. As can be seen from Table 6.1, unemployment is the more prevalent status among the older applicants, no doubt because older men with secure jobs are less likely to make mid-career changes and apply for training. Thus, those older men who do apply are more likely to do so because they are unemployed. However, Table 6.2 shows that relatively few of the older men were *completely* without work for six to twelve months before Government Training. Most of them had mixed spells of employment and unemployment. As for long-term unemployed workers, they are simply not accommodated by the GTCs. It may be a mixture of ignorance (as suggested by Hill), self-rejection, and rejection by the system. The financial incentives for older, lower-paid men run toward claiming SB for as long as possible, since this tends to pay more than Training Allowances. The administrative pressure to look for work appears to diminish as men get older. Once they are into their mid-fifties, the overt pressure is reduced and they no longer need to report weekly to the Employment Service.

TABLE 6.1 Employment Status GTC Trainees, at Application, 1972

Employment Status	Under 40		40 or Older	
	No.	%	No.	%
Unemployed	436	51·1	157	75·8
Occasionally Employed	32	3·8	2	1
Regularly Employed	377	44·2	48	23·2
Don't Know	8	—	—	—
TOTAL	853	100	207	100

Source: Queen Mary College Survey on Government Training Centres (unpublished).

TABLE 6.2 Employment Experience of GTC Trainees Six to Twelve Months before Entry, 1972

Employment Status	Under 40		40 or Older	
	No.	%	No.	%
Always unemployed or sick	20	2·3	11	5·3
Unemployed and Employed	576	67·5	167	80·7
Always Employed	257	30·1	29	14
TOTAL	853	100	207	100

Source: Queen Mary College Survey on Government Training Centres (unpublished).

The logic of the process suggests that a fairly cold-blooded social decision is at play here. A policy goal of raising productivity or curbing aggregate demand will disemploy workers. Older workers will find the labor market adjustment more difficult. If they fall out of the mainstream they become, as Mukerjee has suggested, 'hard luck' cases. It is easier, apparently, to pay them off in Redundancy Benefits and SB, even though this is a form of discard from the productive sector of the economy.

The OECD examiners who studied British manpower policy compared the expenditure of £60 million on redundancy payments for 264,000 workers with the £12 million expenditure on GTCs for 10,000 workers and asked : [17]

> is it socially equitable and economically rational to give most of the money used to alleviate the readjustment of redundant workers to a great number of persons . . . but only very limited sums and incentives to a very limited number of persons for covering expenditure on actual cost and efforts for funding new employment, such as following a training course seeking work in distant areas, or actually moving house?

This imbalance has been somewhat reduced by the growth of GTCs and other training under the Training Opportunities Scheme.

The fact that many unemployed workers, including older ones, are not suitable for training by the strict standards that prevail has troubled some British experts and other interested parties. The problem may be alleviated in the future by the extension of TOPS into semi-skilled occupations with shorter and more simplified training programs than are needed for the skilled occupations. [18]

THE HARD TO EMPLOY

It is difficult to make a fine distinction between those workers who have trouble finding work because of age and the state of the labor market, and those who although physically and mentally fit are characterized as 'hard to employ'. Among the latter are the socially handicapped, the long-term unemployed, and displaced older workers. [19] Facilities exist in Britain that are intended to help such workers, and these are described in the pages that follow.

Industrial Rehabilitation Units (IRUs)

IRUs are workshop-type training centers for disabled persons, operated by the Department of Employment, and form a part of the services offered to disabled persons to help them obtain and keep work. They are of interest to this study because eligibility for industrial rehabilitation is not confined to obviously disabled persons. Their purpose is to give people who 'have been out of employment for a time either because of injury or illness *or for other reasons* a chance to build up their physical capacity for work and . . . their confidence again to work.'[20]

There are twenty-five IRUs in Great Britain, with 2407 places. Twenty-three IRUs are combined with Government Training Centres,[21] although the combination is, in at least some cases, more nominal than real. The emphasis is not on training for a specific skill. Instead, the purpose is to get the client back into the rhythm of work under simulated industrial conditions, and with considerable medical and social work support. An important part of the program is to observe each client carefully and to provide an assessment of his capacity and aptitude for work or further training. Allowances paid to trainees are below the levels of Training Allowances for GTCs, but higher than National Insurance benefits.

Graduates of IRUs are eligible for entry into Government Training Centres, and there is a presumption that further training is one of the options open to them. At the time this study was made there were no data on the number of persons who actually made this transition, but there is reason to believe that it is not very great. The 1968–9 survey of GTC trainees conducted by Hunt, Fox, and Bradley showed that only 2·4 per cent of their sample of trainees came from IRUs,[22] and my rough observations confirm this as a correct order of magnitude.

What we observe here is the categorization of certain long-term unemployed as disabled, and their incorporation into part of the welfare state's mechanism for dealing with the disabled. There seems to be a tendency to classify them as suffering from nervous and mental disabilities, including neurosis, psychosis and mental handicap. Registration as a Disabled Person is voluntary, and the Department of Employment notes that people with mental illness and mental handicap are less likely to register than other disabled persons.[23] Nevertheless, such men and women form one of the two biggest groups of disabled people seeking the Department's services.[24]

Formal status as a disabled person is not needed for entry into an IRU, but the nature of the selection, intake and referral processes is such as to lead to the assumption that there must be something 'wrong' with the client : indeed, why else would he have trouble getting or holding a job? If the client is not physically disabled, mentally retarded, or certifiably psychotic, then the category of 'neurosis' is broad enough to cover what remains.

Not all of the physically fit trainees at IRUs are officially categorized as neurotic, but case-workers tend to dwell on the personal deficiencies and difficulties of such clients. Thus, the test of the labor market becomes an operational test of mental health.

The relative number of physically fit trainees at IRUs has been rising. This may reflect a growth of sophistication in dealing with psychological problems. However, it creates problems for IRUs that are essentially geared to servicing people whose handicap is physical disability. I encountered complaints by the manager of one unit that it had become top heavy with mental problems, drug addicts, schizophrenics and alcoholics whose attitude toward work was poor. It was believed by a number of officials at the operative level that 'genuinely' disabled persons had a better attitude, and were more anxious to succeed. Fear was expressed that the non-disabled would destroy the motivation of the physically handicapped trainees.

The 1973 Employment and Training Act placed IRUs in the Employment Services Agency instead of in the Training Services Agency. The mainstream of government training will be in the latter, and this placement of IRUs suggests that rehabilitation is not considered to be a real manpower training function.

The Socially Disadvantaged

Persons are socially disadvantaged in Britain if they are handicapped in getting work by some non-medical cause such as personality defect or domestic difficulties. This definition, formulated by the Department of Employment, was used in the development of an experiment aimed at identifying such workers in order to give them special help in the placement process.[25] The study took a sample of persons at an Employment Exchange in a poor neighborhood who were unemployed for over three weeks. Using depth interviews, the researchers found that one-third of those who were unemployed for more than three weeks could be classified as socially disadvantaged. Of these, 25 per cent were known to a social work agency, and 80 per cent were receiving Supplementary Benefit.[26] Further study and experimentation has been proposed by the Department of Employment. Among the directions in which action is contemplated is referral of such clients to IRUs.[27]

The Department of Employment clearly accepts responsibility for helping disabled and socially disadvantaged workers to find work. This is a statutory obligation, and there is internal debate over whether to extend its 'resettlement policy'[28] to socially disadvantaged workers and, if so, whether to mix them with the physically and mentally disabled. People who are work-shy are not considered to be socially disabled. The relevant guideline for further proposed experiments states:

it is important that nobody should be initially written off as work-shy. The number of the work-shy is expected to be small and those whose motivation to seek work is undermined by high rates of social security benefits as compared with any rate of pay they can be expected to earn should be excluded as being the responsibility of the Department of Health and Social Security.[29]

The attribution of responsibility for work-shy persons to DHSS is interesting. It suggests that DE is very reluctant about its social work role, and dislikes being the enforcement arm of the welfare state. Indeed, one of the possible reasons for its interest in the socially disadvantaged is to get them out of the regular Employment Exchanges and into special facilities. The Department of Employment (and, presumably, the new Employment Services Agency) is anxious to make its employment service more appealing and competitive with private agencies. To this effect, the management of unemployment benefits will be organized as a service separate from the employment exchanges. This will serve to make the new Employment Service more acceptable to employers and workers by getting the misfits and the benefit claimants out of the way.

Re-establishment Centres
A kind of training establishment for men who are long-term unemployed and long-term claimants of Supplementary Benefits is operated by the Supplementary Benefits Commission. It consists of thirteen Re-establishment Centres[30] created,

> for the re-establishment of persons in need thereof through lack of regular occupation or of instruction or training . . . where . . . such persons may attend or may be maintained by the Supplementary Benefits Commission and . . . may be afforded by the Commission the occupation, instruction or training requisite to fit them for entry into or return to regular employment.[31]

According to the Supplementary Benefits Commission, the purpose of the Centres is to help long-term unemployed men become fit for employment and more acceptable to employers. The area covered begins where the IRUs and GTCs leave off. The underlying theory is that men who have been employed for a long time lose their work habits, and will benefit from a relaxed, unpressurized work environment in which they can become accustomed to getting up in the morning, going to work, mixing with their fellows and completing undemanding tasks (mostly carpentry and metalwork). In this fashion, it is said, the clients can regain sufficient confidence in themselves to obtain and hold jobs when they leave.[32]

The location of Re-establishment in the Supplementary Benefits Commission rather than in the Department of Employment suggests that the Centres are not seriously considered to be part of Britain's manpower training system. Although the notion exists that the Centres might be a link to IRUs and GTCs, very few of the clients make the transition. Men who successfully complete the course are 'routinely' considered for reference to IRUs, but actual referrals are rare. Of the 2291 who were discharged from Re-establishment Centres in 1970, only six men went on to IRUs and none to GTCs.

As was mentioned in Chapter 5, the Centres form part of the control mechanism for inducing men to return to the labor market. The selection process usually originates when Unemployment Review Officers review long-term SB claims and interview claimants to ascertain the reason for claimants' failure to get work. References can also be made by ordinary Review Visitors (case-workers) if they find a man deteriorating. The decision to offer re-establishment is made by the local SB office, subject to confirmation by the Regional Office and by the Centre (if there is a waiting list).

The course varies in length from six to thirteen weeks, depending on an assessment of each clients' needs.[33] The men receive a medical examination upon entry, and physical and mental handicaps are thereby detected. Since the Centres are small, with ten to forty places at a time, the staff has an opportunity to get to know the men. Considerable emphasis is placed on enabling the men to talk, gripe, discuss their grievances against the world, and so forth. There is no positive economic incentive to attend, except for the possible fear of losing Supplementary Benefits.

Reference to the Centre can also be made by the Appeals Tribunal of the Supplementary Benefits Commission in cases where a man is suspected of being work-shy. In 1970, the Tribunal (a sort of appeals court) permitted the Commission to impose re-establishment as a condition for receiving benefits in 157 cases. Thirty-eight men there-

TABLE 6.3 Men Directed to Attend Re-establishment Centres, 1970:
Disposition of Cases

Started work	38
Benefit withdrawn	44
Awaiting further action	7
Being prepared for prosecution	5
Change in circumstances	24
Started course	39
TOTAL	157

Source: Supplementary Benefits Commission.

after went off the rolls and found work. Of eight-three men whose continuation of benefit was conditional on re-establishment, only thirty-nine started the course, and forty-four had their benefits withdrawn. As table 6.3 indicates, the requirement of re-establishment shook more than half the group off the rolls, thus performing the classic function of the workhouse test. The data do not, however, indicate the length of time that the men remained off relief.

Table 6.4 indicates that Re-establishment appears to promote employment activity among its clients. The degree of this activity depends on the state of the labor market. Labor markets were better in 1973 than in 1972. Not surprisingly, more trainees stayed to the completion of the course in 1973 than in the previous year, and more of them found work after completing the course.

It is commonly believed that trainees who attend Re-establishment Centres under compulsion provide a focus of discontent and hinder progress among other men. The manager of a Centre that I visited told me that of four such men who entered in the previous year, three were very disturbed. The only one with potential for being helped was one-eyed and partially disabled. Nevertheless, the SBC believes that,

> the power to make benefits conditional upon attendance is . . . useful in that its existence may influence men who are not in need of re-establishment but who are not making any effort to find work to look around rather harder and obtain work rather than go to a Centre under compulsion.[34]

The lack of follow-up data makes it impossible to say how much of the re-establishment process is useful, and how much consists of 'turning the pile'. It is noteworthy that there is no urge on anyone's part to find out. Formal cost–benefit calculations are impossible; cost figures are not available for Re-establishment Centres because they are combined with Reception Centres (i.e. places for homeless persons). However, attempts are made to keep costs down : workshop supervisors are paid less than their colleagues in GTCs, and are not as skilled. The professional support than can be found in the IRUs is absent. Clearly, a rough and ready decision had been made that a heavy investment in these clients will not pay off.

The idea of offering special labor market services for socially disadvantaged persons has considerable potential, but it has not really been fully explored in Britain. The several services are not even well coordinated, since they fall between two agencies and are popular with neither. What appeared from a distance (i.e. overseas) as an integrated progression from Re-establishment to Industrial Rehabilitation to Government Training turned out, on closer examination, to be more or less separate activities with separate purposes. Government Training is part of a growth oriented manpower policy; in-

dustrial rehabilitation (for the able-bodied) and resettlement are
outside the mainstream of manpower policy. Furthermore, they do
not necessarily serve the function of increasing the earning power of
their clients in the usual human capital sense – i.e. by endowing the
client with a salable skill.

TABLE 6.4 Outcome of Courses at Re-establishment Centres, 1972–3

	1972		1973	
	No.	*%*	*No.*	*%*
Completed the course	1382	60·1	1390	68·3
Failed to complete	919	29·9	645	31·7
TOTAL	2031	100·0	2035	100·0
Experience after completion				
Obtained employment	680	49·2	964	69·4
Remained unemployed	702	50·8	426	30·6
Reasons for non-completion (1972)				
Voluntary dropout	406	44·2		
Sick	315	34·2		
Domestic circumstance	92	10·0		
Physical or mental handicap	55	5·8		
Other	55	5·8		

Source: For 1972, note prepared for the author by the Supplementary
Benefits Commission. 1973 data from Department of Health and Social
Security, *Annual Report 1974* (London: HMSO 1975) p. 83.

Current bureaucratic attitudes in Britain are well represented by
the dialogue between Michael Meacher, a Labour Party member of
parliament, and D. R. F. Turner, Under Secretary of the Treasury
Division, Department of Employment. It is reproduced in its entirety
here so that the full flavor of the thing will not be lost:

Mr. Meacher :   Could I ask whether re-establishment centres
come into the purview of the National Training
Agency.

Mr. Turner :   Rehabilitation Units?

Mr. Meacher :   Not industrial rehabilitation units, re-establishment centres, to re-establish those who, in the
jargon of oratory, are unemployed or who have
lost the habit of work?

Mr. Turner :   These are, I think, centres which are at present
run under the jurisdiction of the Department of
Health and Social Security.

Mr. Meacher :   Yes?

Mr. Turner :   No, these would remain outside the work of the
Agency.

Mr. Meacher : Do you think that is desirable?

Mr. Turner : I have not considered the point, to tell you the truth. I am not in the Department responsible for the centres, and I think really your question ought to be put to that Department in the first place.

Mr. Meacher : Yes, I appreciate that, but since the National Training Agency has been set up to co-ordinate on a much wider scale manpower training, it perhaps is a slight anomaly that this has been left out of the main stream?

Mr. Turner : I would not regard the activities of these centres, insofar as I am acquainted with them, as training. I would not say that they are training people. I would say that they are conditioning people to the idea of employment, and I think that is a very different matter from training.[35]

7 Conclusions and Policy Implications

Manpower training policies are a method of helping persons to acquire skills that are in demand in the labor market. Hence, such policies and programs might be expected to link with the income maintenance programs, in order to help the clients of the latter to achieve a greater degree of economic independence. As has been shown in the foregoing pages, this linkage is weak in Britain, although a potential exists for a stronger relationship. The difficulty stems from (1) a failure to view the motivational forces that operate within the income support system, and (2) the treatment of manpower policies as if they were separate and distinct from issues of income maintenance.

Where the difference between labor market income and income support benefits is sufficiently great, the labor market does its own motivational job, at least when it offers sufficient employment. (The qualification needs to be stressed, since high unemployment generates its own needs for relief payments.) The poverty prone population among the able-bodied are characterized by a low potential earning power. If work does not yield all that much more than welfare, the motive to seek and hold a job will be blunted. This is an especially insidious poverty trap, because it keeps people quietly tucked away in the bottom of the income distribution.

To the first generation of immigrants from an underdeveloped country or region, the low end of the labor market may look inviting as compared to conditions back home. Migrants also bring with them the hope of upward mobility, for themselves or for their children. Thus, for a time, the low-wage jobs in the economy may be filled, and the presence of this labor supply may perpetuate the low-wage sector. However, the children of the migrants may not behave this way if poor education and racial barriers have kept them socially and economically disadvantaged. Instead, they will behave like the rest of the indigenous population. The 'dirty' jobs at low pay being uninviting, they will tend to make better use of income support facilities than did their parents. This has been the experience in the United States with migrants who moved from the agricultural regions in the American South and Puerto Rico into the northern and western industrial cities. The new source of labor for American low-pay service jobs are immigrants, many of them illegal, from Mexico, the Caribbean, and South America. This pattern is not unfamiliar to British readers, who may find a somewhat parallel situation with New Commonwealth immigrants.

It would seem important, therefore, to provide avenues of upward mobility to the more chronically impoverished segments of the population. The absence of such opportunities can lead to the development of a more or less permanent underclass. This group will receive additional recruits from among workers who are discarded by the industrial process as a result of economic and technological change. Considerations of humanity, as well as of political stability, require that the population so discarded be supported by the rest of the community. The same considerations, however, suggest that such people be given the opportunity to move from the bottom of the income distribution and into the mainstream of the community.

If an economy is oriented toward economic growth, then a dispassionate economic view of the long-term or chronically unemployed adult population treats them as a wasted stock of human resources. Efficient use of human resources is, after all, the underlying rationale of manpower services. Ironically, socialist planners seem to be more conscious of the need to economize human resources than are capitalist policy-makers. The former are far less tolerant than we are of an idle population; generous income support is a capitalist luxury.

Policies that are designed to enable people to move from welfare dependence to independent status must consider the nature and functioning of income maintenance policies together with the nature and functioning of manpower policies. An analysis of this interaction has been attempted here with respect to Britain. The conclusions that emerge that are policy-relevent to both Britain and the United States are summarized below.

INCOME MAINTENANCE

All income maintenance programs contain policies regarding the labor market behavior of their clients. Such policies may be explicitly stated, but there is always a set of policies that are implicit in the structure of sanctions and incentives – the pushes and pulls – that make up the practices and the benefits of the system. When the ex-

D

plicit and implicit policies conflict, it is the latter that govern. The reality that the client faces is not the broad mandate of the legislature but the specific rules developed by the agency and administered by the individuals who comprise the bureaucratic structure. This point may be overlooked in policy debates over whether a particular category of client should or should not be induced (or compelled) to enter the labor market. An operative policy may actually be in effect that is not obvious to observers.

This can be illustrated with an example from the American experience with AFDC, where benefits are based on each state's standard of need. Prior to 1967, the official policy that pertained to earned income was that it reduced benefits by the same amount, i.e. a 100 per cent tax was levied on earnings. In practice, however, a number of states paid benefits well below their standard of need, but did not reduce benefits in the face of earned income until the combination of benefits and earnings were equal to the standard of need. Accordingly, the real policy in such states was to encourage earnings in the part-time or low-wage end of the labor market, and the effective tax rate for this range of earnings was zero. The states in question were largely low-benefit southern states, and their informal administrative practices were to add compulsion to the incentive.[1] These practices went largely unnoticed in Congressional debates, which centered heavily on the iniquities of the 100 per cent tax rate on earnings and reformed it by substituting the provision that recipients could retain the first $30 per month plus 33 per cent of the balance, after disregarding work-related expenses.

The new official policy led to as many implicit policy variations as the old one. Some states define work-related expenses narrowly, and limit them. Others define them broadly, and place few limits on them. The average tax on earnings thus varies considerably from state to state for an AFDC family of a given size, as does the marginal tax rate applicable to any level of earnings. The result is that the actual impact of earnings on benefits simply cannot be inferred from the explicit policy that was legislated.[2]

For analytic purposes, it is necessary to examine all of the components of a national income maintenance system and not merely one program in the set. The various programs, although developed for different purposes, can interact with one another, *both when they are additive and when they are mutually exclusive.* When viewed together, the set of programs presents a structure of incentives and disincentives. If the structure is not coordinated, it may encourage behavior on the part of clients that is not necessarily in keeping with the explicit goals of any one program.

The impact of additive benefit programs has been the subject of

considerable discussion both in Britain and in America. The high
marginal tax rates that are referred to in the debate on the poverty
trap in Chapter 4 come from the availability of multiple benefits,
where a small earnings increase can lead to a relatively large loss of
total benefits. Less attention has been paid to the interaction of
mutually exclusive benefits. These interact when the present different
alternatives that may be available to the claimant.

This proposition can be illustrated with reference to Family
Income Supplement and Supplementary Benefit in Britain. The
two benefits are mutually exclusive. Explicit British policy is that
unsupported mothers are free to raise their children (as best they
can) on SB if they have no other means of support, and are not
compelled to seek work. Work is an alternative to SB as a source of
income, but the earnings alternative for most of the relevant population is likely to be low, especially net of child care costs. However,
the enactment of FIS has made work a viable alternative for a segment of this population, and has attracted a relatively large clientele
of female household heads in Britain.

A high ratio of benefit income to potential labor market income
puts a relatively great burden on the administrative devices and
control measures used to induce or compel a return to the labor
market. The transfer cost of an incentive-orientated high-benefit
system, such as a generous negative income tax, is very great, even
without reference to the real costs that might be generated by lost
output. The obverse of this is that means-tested systems can afford
to maintain income at higher levels, given the society's willingness
to make income transfers of a given size, by concentrating benefits
on the target population.

Means tests and other benefit selection modes have their own costs,
both economic and politico-social. Resources are absorbed in the task
of investigating claimants. Complex rules are developed for complex
cases, and these bring forth further needs for investigation, cross-
checking facts, and judging the motivations and behaviors of particular clients. The bureaucratic structures that are developed for
these tasks become cumbersome : they grow large in absolute size
and cost, and are not noted for their cost-effectiveness with regard
to specific objectives. Some of the costs are hidden because they are
shifted to the claimants : the time spent waiting in line that might be
better spent in child care or job search; the consequence of poor
judgment by a case officer that deprives a client of income; the psy-
chic cost of harassment of humiliation to the honest claimant who is
maltreated by a stupid or punitive case-worker. These are real
economic costs in that they diminish the real welfare of members of
the community.

The alternatives to means tests are commonly believed to be all-inclusive and universal income guarantees with negative tax features. Their principal drawbacks are well known by now. A tax rate low enough to serve as an incentive spreads eligibility too far up on the income scale. An income guarantee that is high enough for social decency would have a powerful work disincentive – or so it is feared – even with a relatively low negative tax rate. It is noteworthy that neither the British nor the American tax proposals (Tax Credits and Family Assistance Plan, respectively) were genuine substitutes for public assistance to persons out of work. The former excluded Supplementary Benefits, while the latter retained the means test and work requirement.

Accordingly, administrative sanctions are likely to remain imbedded in an income maintenance system. Whatever the drawbacks of this may be, it enables needy families without resources or employment to receive support at income levels that are closer to the society's social minimum than might otherwise be the case.

When unemployment is high, administrative sanctions are of limited effectiveness, especially with respect to claimants whose employability and earnings capacity are curtailed by reason of age, obsolescent skill, prejudice, or social disadvantage. However, the bureaucracy may be under political pressure to apply some controls in any event. The targets are likely to be the 'least deserving' of the claimants, that is, those that are least favored in the political and social judgment of the society. This role seems to be played in Britain by unskilled men below the age of forty-five, in that they are subjected to greater pressures than skilled men who receive SB. It is useful to temper the policy with some realism, however, and this can be done by varying the pressure of the control devices in response to the state of the labor market. In Britain, for example, the 'four-week rule' that requires unskilled men to reapply for benefits at the end of every four weeks is suspended in areas of high unemployment. No formal equivalent to this sort of policy exists in the United States. The pressures applied to Unemployment Insurance claimants tend to fall off in periods of high unemployment, partly because the press of business prevents personnel from devoting much time to any one claimant.

However, the nature of the financing of public assistance benefits in the United States paradoxically increases the motivation of welfare officials to be harsh during periods of high unemployment. High unemployment is associated with declining state and local tax revenues at the same time that it causes the case-load to rise. Hence, the pressures to economize mount, commonly at the expense of the 'less deserving' poor. If the central government is also intent on curbing the growth of social outlays (as was the case in the United States in 1975), then administrative sanctions will be encouraged in the programs for less favored people that are subject to the direct or indirect control of the central government.

This leads to dysfunctional behavior by the income maintenance system at the public assistance level. In 1975, the US Department of Agriculture's response to increased food stamp applications led to an observable increase in the tightening of eligibility standards in what appeared to be a conscious attempt to discourage new clients and thus to reduce outlays on food stamps.

MANPOWER SERVICES

If our analysis is correct, then income maintenance systems in the future are likely to retain a variety of sanctions and control mechanism. One purpose of such mechanisms will be to induce or even compel claimants to engage in approved labor market behavior, that is, to look for work and, if possible, to find and hold jobs. The control mechanisms in both countries have had a well-deserved reputation for arbitrariness and, in some cases, cruelty.[3] As such (they have been the proper target for humanitarian reform.

A way to relieve the burden on the control mechanisms is to raise the opportunity cost to claimants of remaining on welfare. Obviously, this can be done by reducing the real value of the benefits. Where benefits are set at society's estimate of minimal social decency, this course of action has little to commend it. Another way to raise the opportunity cost of staying on the dole is to raise the potential earning powers of claimants, or at least some portion of them, by the use of manpower training programs and supportive services.

Manpower policies can be oriented primarily toward the achievement of economic growth goals. Alternatively, policies can be directed toward the social policy goals of assisting the poorer segments of the population. It is often believed that the two goals are mutually inconsistent, in that the presence of long-term unemployed and other trainees with special problems will 'contaminate' other trainees very much the way disadvantaged students can reduce the educational standards of a school. Where productivity and growth are principal goals, the incentive structure faced by training managers will cause them to select trainees with high success probabilities. Indicators of success are calculated in terms of trainees who complete their courses and are placed in jobs. The training enterprise, be it a Government Training Centre, an Industry Training Board, or whatever, justifies its existence by the common criteria of efficient use of resources. The resource cost of sustaining a hard-to-train worker does not appear on its accounts.

As a result, economically oriented manpower policies will tend to slough off 'hard luck cases' as something to be dealt with by another branch of government. The use of cost–benefit analysis as a policy tool reinforces this tendency. Benefits are calculated as the present value of the trainees' additional earnings attributable to the training process. Costs are the implicit and explicit outlays on the training process itself. The younger the trainees, the greater the potential benefits, since young trainees have more working time left in their lives. The more adept the trainees, the lower the cost of training them. The excess of benefits over costs constitutes a sort of social profit, although it is not clear how this 'profit' is distributed in the economy.

This is not to say that cost–benefit analysis is pointless. To the contrary, it is often a useful technique for judging a carefully defined policy whose purpose is to increase output. But for the same reason, it does not lend itself to the exploration of conflicts and trade-off possibilities between the social (including redistributive) goals and the economic goals of a manpower policy. Such an exploration can nevertheless be useful, even if it must, of necessity, be made in qualitative terms.

The usual approach to employment and training programs for 'hard' cases is to segregate them from programs that are tied to the mainstream of labor markets. In the United States, the training effort under the pre-1973 programs (i.e. before the Comprehensive Employment and Training Act which relegated training to state programs) was heavily directed at the poor and disadvantaged. There were five major programs: Manpower Development and Training Act (MDTA), Neighborhood Youth Corps (NYC), Job Corps, Job Opportunities in the Business Sector (JOBS), and the Work Incentive Program (WIN) for AFDC recipients. Of these, only MDTA served a clientele that was not exclusively disadvantaged. Not surprisingly, its performance in benefit–cost terms seems to have been better than that of other programs. More to the point, it was relatively effective for the disadvantaged, i.e. poor persons who were either (1) school dropouts, (2) members of minority groups, (3) under twenty-two years of age, (4) over forty-five, or (5) handicapped.[4] MDTA was the closest American approximation of a mainstream training scheme, one whose purpose it is to feed persons into primary labor markets.

The evidence on the other programs – those devoted exclusively to disadvantaged workers – while not very conclusive because of the poor quality of the available information, has not been very encouraging.[5] Those programs aimed exclusively at the young disadvantaged have had a reputation for being disguised income maintenance programs, both for their trainees and for the trainers. Whatever the social value of such income maintenance may be, it does little to alter the long-run earning powers of the trainees. The JOBS program, in which private enterprises received subsidies for training disadvantaged workers, was widely subverted by firms that used it to obtain cheap labor for relatively unskilled tasks.[6] Even where intentions are good, the jobs are low-pay jobs with few opportunities for improvement.

Britain, unlike the United States, has had mainstream training programs in the form of Government Training Centres and Industrial Training Boards. These, and an expanded Training Opportunities Scheme, are now under the jurisdiction of the Manpower Services Commission and its Training Services Agency. They retain their orientation toward recruiting persons most likely to succeed, with bias against the long-term unemployed. These persons and other 'hard cases' are left to training schemes such as Industrial Rehabilitation Units and Re-establishment Centres. IRUs, it will be recalled, were not originally intended to serve physically able-bodied men. An able-bodied trainee who enters into such a program is, by definition, neurotic, psychotic or retarded. None of these labels make him appealing to potential employers. Indeed, such a trainee is not even appealing to those who manage the mainstream training programs.

Out-of-the-mainstream manpower programs may serve as part of the control mechanism of an income maintenance policy.[7] In this respect, they perform the classic Poor Law functions of the workhouse test, i.e. (1) to be an alternative that is less desirable to the client than work (always assuming that work is available), and (2) to prevent the client from secretly working while collecting assistance payments. However useful these functions may be, they should not be confused with the training of persons for work in the open labor market.

In the United States the Work Incentive Program (WIN) for AFDC recipients was intended to 'shake out' AFDC recipients through the process of registration, evaluation, and referral to work or training. The training aspect of WIN has never been successful, despite the good intentions of many trainers and trainees. In the early years of its operation, WIN had a 'Potemkin Village effect' in persuading the public and even some clients that something was being done about a problem. As is often the case with cardboard programs, disillusionment has set in.

The present variant on WIN called WIN II, emphasizes direct placement of welfare recipients. Employers who hire and keep welfare recipients for two years receive a credit of 20 per cent of the first year's wages against their taxes. In fiscal year 1973, the bulk of the 25,000 recipients for whom tax credits were granted were employed in jobs at or near the legal minimum wage, in unskilled clerical or service occupations.[8] As for the rest of the WIN II job placements, 52 per cent were employed for less than ninety days.[9] This indicates the presence of what the British call 'turning the pile'.[10] It is difficult for a man in the United States to support a family at a wage of $2·10 per hour (88 pence) if he has, say, 120 hours of work per month. His monthly income, after deducting social security tax, would come to $237·26 (or £99). He would be entitled to purchase food stamps that add $100·75 to his income, for a total monthly income of $338·01 (£140). On welfare (in New York City), the family income would be $412 per month (including the value of food stamps) *plus housing costs* of $150 to $300 per month, or more. It would not be astonishing if men on such part-time, low-wage jobs felt no powerful urge to remain at work.

As shown above in the operation of WIN II for men, the use of manpower services as work test devices may not be effective with respect either to the explicit goal of the service (training and place-ment) or its implicit goal as a control mechanism. However, this may not be apparent from raw data on the number of clients pro-cessed. Similarly, the British use of IRUs and Re-establishment Centres gives a deceptive view that something by way of manpower services are being offered to abled-bodied but hard-to-employ per-sons. As a practical matter, it is difficult is evaluate them even as control devices, and one concludes that a 'Potemkin Village' effect may in part, be operative.

POLICY IMPLICATIONS

Britain has the elements of a graduated structure of training services that could be of real value to the long-term unemployed and to others who have been barred or discarded from the mainstream of the labor market. The IRUs and Re-establishment Centres can serve as threshold training services to feed successful graduates of these programs into the larger Training Opportunities Scheme. Existing concepts of rehabilitation and re-establishment might bear re-exam-ination. Experimentation may be worthwhile with training structures that begin with basic education (where needed) and move trainees by degrees into more complex and directly salable skills.

Americans, on the other hand, may wish to reconsider the assump-tion that the best way of increasing the employability of the hard to employ is to provide programs aimed exclusively at this popula-tion. Although the training and further education opportunities for most American adults now lie outside the scope of organized man-power policy, they fall within the scope of various government subsidies. A fruitful direction for policy might be the better use of such private and public facilities by disadvantaged persons. Alternatively, the social goal of helping the disadvantaged might be served by a better organization of training and educational opportunities for all workers, with a renewed emphasis on the economic goals of such a policy, since this is more likely to help persons return to the primary labor market.

In both countries, the *de facto* structure of incentives and controls (the pushes and pulls referred to in Chapter 4) bear re-examination for consonance with the goals of each income maintenance system. Where the goal is to return people to self-sufficient status, the incentive structure should favor labor market participation. A policy that expects people to behave irrationally is a foolish policy. Incentives, by themselves, cannot move the harder to employ into decent employment. It is the combination of training, supportive services, information, and a consonant incentive structure that can help people who have been side-tracked in the labor market to become self-sufficient. The greater the incentives, the less the call for the use of administrative measures that are, at heart, overt forms of compulsion.

Microeconomic policies are not sufficient, however. They must be complemented by macroeconomic policies that maintain high employment. Lord Beveridge understood this, as did the founding fathers of the American social security system. The potential contribution of manpower policies to this goal has never been fully exploited. In the present economic turmoil of the industrial economies, it has become fashionable to give increasingly greater preference to high unemployment and low rates of economic growth as the policy tools for price stability. It is safe to say that the remedies for an economy that cannot, over the longer term, fully employ its population of working age are likely to be more drastic than a mere restructuring of manpower and income support policies. We are, in the final analysis, talking about our ability to make full use of the community's human resources in order to produce goods and services for the community's welfare, to be distributed in some accordance with the community's notion of distributive justice. That is what we do when we use policy to alter or replace the actions of markets. Distributive justice is a political goal. Policy is a political tool. It might as well be used as effectively as we know how.

Appendix to Chapter 2: Major US Income Maintenance Programs

Below are summarized the major American public programs in social insurance and public assistance. It should be kept in mind that in the United States, more than in Britain, reliance is placed on private income maintenance schemes, such as collectively bargained pension and health plans. To simplify matters, I have excluded special programs for armed forces veterans, federal civil servants, Cuban refugees, coal-miners, Indians, and education grants. Also excluded are experimental schemes, such as housing allowances (rent rebates) that are available to a relatively small number of people.

SOCIAL INSURANCE PROGRAMS

Social Security Administration
Old Age, Survivors and Disability Insurance. This provides monthly pensions for retired workers and their dependents, survivors caring for minor children, and workers (and their dependents) where the worker becomes totally disabled. To be eligible, the worker must be 'insured' for a requisite number of years, i.e. have been employed in jobs covered by the system. Benefits are earnings-related, subject to a minimum and a maximum, so that low-wage-earners receive relatively higher benefits. Furthermore, benefits are adjusted twice yearly for changes in the Consumer Price Index. Financing is through a payroll tax of 11·7 per cent of earnings up to $14,100, divided equally between employer and worker. Self-employed persons pay 8 per cent of earnings up to $14,100.
Medicare. This is national health insurance for elderly and totally disabled persons. The scheme consists of two parts, Hospital Insurance (HI) and Supplementary Medical Insurance (SMI). Virtually all of the aged are covered by HI, without reference to previous

payroll tax contributions, and HI payments are made from a trust fund financed by one percentage point of the Social Security tax (see above). SMI covers other medical expenses, and is available to retired and disabled persons covered by Social Security. It is financed by premiums paid by such persons, plus a contribution from the general revenues of the federal government.

State Programs
Unemployment Insurance. Benefits are payable to persons who have lost their jobs, generally only for economic reasons. Eligibility requirements vary from state to state. The usual length of the benefit period is twenty-six weeks, with a thirteen-week extension in states with high rates of unemployment. A temporary emergency extension of another twenty-six weeks is scheduled to expire in 1977. Benefits are financed by payroll taxes levied on employers .The temporary extension is financed out of general federal revenues. Benefits are earnings-related, subject to minimum and maximum payments. A number of states make additional payments for dependents.
Workmen's Compensation. Each state has its own industrial injuries scheme. Generally speaking, benefits encompass medical expenses for illnesses and injuries caused by employment, compensation for permanent injuries, and income support (usually at levels of the state's unemployment benefit rate) for the period of the disability. Employers covered by the scheme purchase insurance, largely from private insurance carriers. A number of states have funds that compete with private carriers. Workmen's Compensation benefits may be added to Disability Insurance benefits of the Social Security program (see above).

PUBLIC ASSISTANCE
Public assistance programs are administered by states or localities, except as noted below, with varying degrees of federal subvention on cost-sharing bases. Supplemental Security Income, Food Stamps and the National School Lunch Program are federal schemes with uniform minimum benefits and eligibility requirements. AFDC and Medicaid are federal–state programs (in ten states, federal–state–local), subject to a certain amount of federal control. All programs are means-tested.

Cash Benefits
Aid to Families with Dependent Children. Assistance is provided to needy families with dependent children where the father is absent, incapacitated or (in twenty-five states) unemployed. Benefits are based on the standard of need by family size estimated by each state, but states may pay less than 100 per cent of their own standard.

Federal contributions range from 50 per cent to 83 per cent of costs, depending on each state's level of income. Adult recipients are required to register for work or training, although the great majority are not under a *de facto* compulsion. Recipients who earn wage income may retain benefits to the extent of (1) their work expenses, (2) $30 per month, and (3) one-third of the balance of their earnings. The program for unemployed male heads of households (AFDC–UP) differs in that recipients become disqualified for benefits if they work in excess of 100 hours per month. Food stamps may be used to supplement AFDC benefits.

Supplemental Security Income. Cash benefits are available for the indigent aged and disabled. The benefit level is based on family size and is not adjustable for housing costs or other specific variations in need. Recipients are not eligible for food stamps. Social Security benefits are fully deductible from SSI, except that SSI recipients can retain a small minimum benefit. Earned income leads to a benefit loss at the rate of 50 per cent. The minimum benefit level, by family size, is established by federal legislation and is federally financed. States whose benefits were higher when the program was enacted in 1974 must supplement the benefits to maintain the higher levels. States may administer the program or contract out administration to the Social Security Administration.

General Assistance. The catch-all term for state and local programs used to aid persons who are not eligible for any other category of assistance. Some states and localities also use GA to supplement other types of assistance. Programs are financed out of state and local revenues. Some states have no official GA programs.

In-Kind Benefits

Food Stamps. These are vouchers with face values of $1 and $10. Persons with low assets and with incomes below the prescribed maximum net incomes (varying by family size) may purchase food stamps below their face value, provided that they spend 22·5 per cent of family income on the stamps. The stamps may be used to purchase American-produced food at most food stores. The difference between the cost of the food stamps and their par value is, in effect, a low income supplement with a benefit–loss rate of 22·5 per cent.

School Lunches. The US Department of Agriculture makes cash and commodity grants to schools for their use in providing free or reduced-price school lunches to needy children. Participation by the state or local school authorities is voluntary.

Medical Assistance (Medicaid). Vendor payments for medical care are made for persons who receive public assistance cash benefits. In a number of states, persons who are 'medically indigent' are also eligible. For the aged and disabled, Medicaid can be used to supplement Medicare in payment of insurance premiums and in providing services not covered by Medicare, such as long-term care in nursing homes.

Public Housing. Housing units are available to certain needy families and individuals, at below market rents, in 2286 localities in the United States. Rents are related to household income, and families in public housing whose incomes rise above the prescribed maxima must find other accommodations. Local housing authorities receive financial assistance from the federal government.

Legal Services. Federal grants are made to local Legal Aid Societies and other voluntary non-profit groups to provide legal services in civil cases for indigent clients. Indigent persons charged with crimes are constitutionally entitled to legal representation; in such cases, the court appoints lawyers. In some states the task of defending indigents charged with offenses is performed by states agencies called Public Defenders.

MANPOWER-RELATED PROGRAMS

As noted in the text, income maintenance is an important function of manpower programs in the United States. There is no uniform scale of allowances. Under the Comprehensive Employment and Training Act of 1973, Federal grants are made to states and localities for training schemes and subsidized employment. The most explicit income support schemes under the manpower rubric are :

Neighborhood Youth Corps

These are local projects that help (1) provide part-time work for needy students, (2) provide summer jobs during school vacations, and (3) provide work training or other services to school drop-outs.

Public Employment Programs

During the past two recessions, temporary federal subsidies have been provided to local governments for the purpose of providing work for unemployed persons. Public Employment programs are not, at this time, part of the permanent structure of income support in the United States. Some local governments appear to be using federal manpower program funds in order to rehire some of their redundant employees.

SOURCES

(US Department of Health, Education and Welfare, Social Security Administration, *Social Security Programs in the United States* (Washington : US Government Printing Office, 1974); US Congress, Joint Economic Committee, Studies in Public Welfare No. 20, *Handbook of Public Income Transfer Programs: 1975* (Washington : US Government Printing Office, 1974).

Appendix to Chapter 3: Major British Income Maintenance Programs

NATIONAL INSURANCE
This is the backbone of the British social insurance system, and corresponds roughly to the American notion of social security. All prime-age adults are required to participate by the payment of contributions (i.e. taxes). Employed workers have their contributions withheld from their pay, and employers are also required to contribute. Additional funds for the system come from the Exchequer out of general revenues. Benefits are generally based on family size and composition, and some of them pay an earnings-related supplement for the first six months. Where benefits fall below the poverty line, they may be supplemented by Supplementary Benefits (see below). The principal programs relevant to employable adults are :

Unemployment Benefit
Payable for unemployment of from two days to one year at the standard rate. Earnings-related benefits are payable from the thirteenth day to six months. Total benefits cannot exceed 85 per cent of usual earnings. Married women who have chosen to contribute at a lower rate than men do not qualify.

Sickness and Invalidity Benefit
Payable for illness of from three days to one year at the same rate as Unemployment Benefit. After 168 working days it is supplemented by Invalidity Benefit at a rate that declines with the claimant's age.

Maternity Benefits
All women are eligible for a grant of £25 per child per confinement. Working women who are pregnant can receive a weekly allowance equal to the standard unemployment benefit for single men for

a period beginning eleven weeks before confinement and ending six weeks after confinement.

Retirement Pension
Available to men at age sixty-five and women at age sixty who work no more than twelve hours weekly and earn less than a small prescribed amount. Earnings limitation ceases at 70 and 65, respectively. Payable at the same standard rate as other benefits, but a graduated amount is payable to those who chose to pay an additional contribution. The system is currently shifting over to greater emphasis on employer pension plans.

Widows' Benefits
All widows receive an allowance for twenty-six weeks following the death of their husband, at the standard rate plus earnings-related benefits. Widows with dependent children receive a widowed mothers' allowance with benefits for each minor child. At the expiration of the allowance, widows over forty can continue to receive a small pension.

INDUSTRIAL INJURIES
This is essentially the British version of Workmen's Compensation. It is financed by contributions levied on employees and employers, and further subsidized by the Exchequer. Benefits may be supplemented by Supplementary Benefits. The principal benefits are :

Injury Benefit
Payable up to twenty-six weeks. The basic rate is higher than the rate for sickness benefit.

Disablement Benefit
Based on medical assessment of the extent of claimant's injury, from 20 per cent disability (paid with lump sum) to 100 per cent, plus additions for various situations such as unemployability, unfitness to return to regular job, need for constant supervision, etc. Payment of the above pension does not necessarily disqualify claimants from National Insurance benefits.

Death Benefits For Widows and Dependents
Allowances for minor children at the standard rate of NI, and a twenty-six week allowance and pension similar to NI Widows' Benefit. Widows receiving such benefits are not eligible for NI Widows' Benefits.

FAMILY ALLOWANCES

Families with two or more more children receive a weekly allowance of 90 pence for the first two children and £1 for each additional child. The allowance is financed entirely by the Exchequer out of general revenues, and is paid directly to the mother where possible. Benefits are taxable as ordinary income. There is no means test or other condition of eligibility. However, Supplementary Benefits are paid net of Family Allowances.

FAMILY INCOME SUPPLEMENT

Payable to families with incomes below a sort of poverty scale based on family size. The benefit pays 50 per cent of the difference between actual income and the designated amount of the scale, up to a maximum of £7.50 per week, and is financed out of general revenues. Claimants are automatically eligible for certain other welfare benefits, such as free eyeglasses, dental treatment, school meals, etc.

SUPPLEMENTARY BENEFITS (Supplementary Benefits Commission, Department of Health and Social Security)

This is the basic public assistance program, financed by the Exchequer out of general revenues. Claimants are automatically eligible for certain other benefits, such as free eyeglasses, prescriptions, dental treatment, school meals, etc. Rent and rate rebates must be claimed, and are subtracted from benefits.

Supplementary Allowance

To bring family resources up to the 'appropriate level of requirements' set by Parliament, for persons below pensionable age, i.e. a poverty line. Thus, benefits are means-tested. A scale of payments exists, based on family size and age of children, plus housing costs and exceptional needs. SB cannot be used to supplement full-time earnings (see FIS), and part-time earnings above £2 per week are taxed at 100 per cent. Benefits cannot exceed full-time earnings in claimant's usual occupation (wage stop). Employable claimants must register for work, except mothers caring for minor children.

Supplementary Pension

Essentially the same thing for persons of pensionable age.

MISCELLANEOUS LOCAL AUTHORITY WELFARE BENEFITS

Council Housing

Local authorities build and maintain public housing for local residents, subject to a rather generous needs test. The last government directed authorities to move all rents up toward competitive levels.

Rent Rebates and Allowances
Rent subsidies administered at local level and income-tested, with implicit marginal tax rates of 17–25 per cent.

Rate Rebates
Income-tested reductions in local property taxes.

Free School Meals
Remission of the charge for school lunches for poor children.

Higher Education Grants
Maintenance grants to students in higher education, income-tested to parents.

DEPARTMENT OF EMPLOYMENT BENEFITS
A number of cash benefits are administered by the Department of Employment and the Training Services Agency as part of their responsibilities for British manpower policy. The principal ones are :

Redundancy Payments
Lump sum payments to workers dismissed for economic reasons. The amount is a function of length of service and the age during which the service was performed. Payments are made by the employer, but half the payment is then recouped from a fund which is financed by a payroll tax on employers.

Training Allowances
Weekly allowances to trainees under the Training Opportunities Scheme, at Government Training Centres or Colleges of Further Education. The scale is similar to NI benefits, but slightly higher. Allowances are slightly lower for Industrial Rehabilitation.

Employment Transfer Scheme
Benefits to aid workers to move to another locality because of actual or impending unemployment. The program is limited to workers who earn less than £2650 per year. Benefits include payment of fare to the job interview, a small weekly allowance while the worker's family remains at the old home, cost of moving personal effects, a lump sum toward incidental expenses, and aid in selling and buying the home. Special benefits exist for movement into less developed ('assisted') areas. The purpose is to promote labor mobility, but the numbers involved have been small.

SOURCES
British Information Services, *Social Security in Britain* (London : British Information Services, 1973) pp. 10–38; A. Harding Boulton, *Law and Practice of Social Security* (Bristol : Jordan & Sons, 1972); Department of Health and Social Security, *A Guide to Social Security* (Nov 1969), and *Supplementary Benefits Handbook,* Supplementary Benefits Administration Papers, 2 (London : HMSO, Nov 1972); Family Welfare Association, *Guide to the Social Services* (London : MacDonald & Evans, 1973) pp. 112–79; Tony Lynes, *The Penguin Guide to Supplementary Benefits* (Harmondsworth, Middlesex : Penguin, 1972); Phyllis Willmott, *Public Social Services* (London : Bedford Square Press, 1973) pp. 17–83.

Notes

CHAPTER 1

1. Harold L. Wilensky, *The Welfare State and Equality* (Berkeley: University of California Press, 1974) pp. 30–1.
2. Ibid., p. xi.
3. P. R. Kaim-Caudle, *Comparative Social Policy and Social Security: A Ten Country Study* (New York: Dunellen, 1973).
4. English parishes (i.e. local governments) that used the Speenhamland System in effect broadened relief of the able-bodied into an income guarantee based on family size and the price of bread, subject to a means test and a work requirement. As often occurs in policy crises, much of the discussion in 1834 was beside the point, since the Speenhamland System was never as widespread as had been supposed and in 1834 was no longer operative in most of England. See M. Blaug, 'The Myth of the Old Poor Law', *Journal of Economic History,* 23 (Jun 1963) p. 158.
5. Mary Barnett Gilson, *Unemployment Insurance in Great Britain* (New York: Industrial Relations Counselors, 1931) p. 289.
6. Ibid., pp. 289–90. Also see T. S. Chegwidden and G. Myrddin-Evans, *The Employment Exchange Service of Great Britain* (New York: Industrial Relations Counselors, 1934) pp. 144–56.
7. The United States has no statistical series to measure job vacancies.
8. AFDC is the principal American public assistance program for fatherless families and, in some states, for intact families where the father is unemployed but without unemployment compensation. GA is a set of public assistance programs for able-bodied persons who are not eligible for AFDC. See Chapter 2 for a description of American social insurance and public assistance programs. For a good history of US manpower policy, see Sar A. Levitan, Garth L. Mangum and Ray Marshall, *Human Resources and Labor Markets* (New York: Harper and Row, 1972) pp. 299–340.

CHAPTER 2

1. Or fraction thereof, if the state pays less than 100 per cent of its own standard of need.
2. For an excellent summary of UI and other social insurance programs, see US Department of Health, Education and Welfare, Social Security Administration, *Social Security Programs in the United States* (Washington: US Government Printing Office, 1973).
3. Bruno Stein, *On Relief: The Economics of Poverty and Public Welfare* (New York: Basic Books, Inc., 1971) pp. 43–9.
4. A complete listing of federal benefit programs can be found in Joint Economic Committee, 93rd Congress, *Studies in Public Welfare,* Paper No. 14 (Washington: US Government Printing Office, 1974) pp. 45–54.
5. US Department of Health, Education and Welfare, Social Security

Administration, *Social Security Programs in the United States, op cit.*, p. 31.

6. Frances F. Piven and Richard Cloward, *Regulating the Poor: The Functions of Public Welfare* (New York: Pantheon, 1971).

7. The National Welfare Rights Organization is a group that seeks to organize welfare recipients, to protect their rights, and to lobby for improved benefits. A somewhat similar organization in Britain is the Child Poverty Action Group.

8. Bruno Stein, 'Poverty and the Present Welfare System', in *Welfare: A National Policy* (Los Angeles: Institute of Industrial Relations, University of California, 1973) p. 17.

9. For a thorough discussion of this subject, see the essays in US Congress, Joint Economic Committee, Studies in Public Welfare No. 12, *The Family, Poverty and Welfare Programs* (Washington: US Government Printing Office, 1973 and 1974) parts II and III.

10. For example, see the calculation by M. Cox as reported in P. S. Albin and B. Stein, 'The Constrained Demand for Public Assistance', *Journal of Human Resources* (Summer 1968) pp. 310–11. Barbara Boland estimates that 63 per cent of eligible families headed by women received AFDC and that by 1970 participation climbed to 90 per cent. B. Boland, 'Participation in the AFDC Program', Studies in Public Welfare no. 12, op. cit., p. 153.

11. Charles C. Killingsworth, 'Employment as an Alternative to Welfare', in *Welfare: A National Policy,* pp. 45–7. Note that while Killingsworth's 'split-level' labor market resembles the dual labor market thesis, the two concepts do not fully coincide. An excellent attempt to summarize the reasons for the growth in welfare dependency in one place – New York City – is found in Larry A. Jackson and William A. Johnson, *Protest By the Poor* (New York: NYC Rand Institute, Aug 1973) pp. 223–41.

12. Peter S. Albin and Bruno Stein, 'Determinants of Relief Policy at the Sub-Federal Level', *Southern Economic Journal,* vol. XXXVIII (Apr 1971) pp. 445–57.

13. I am not here discussing the economics of the labor supply and the questions of income and leisure with respect to it. The concern is with the politics of the issue, and the reader is reminded that political behavior, unlike economic behavior, can be non-rational.

14. See Sar. A. Levitan, Martin Rein, and David Marwick, *Work and Welfare Go Together* (Baltimore: Johns Hopkins University Press) pp. 26–35.

15. US Department of Labor, 'Children of Working Mothers, March 1973', Special Labor Force Report 165, *Monthly Labor Review* (May 1974).

16. Bruno Stein, 'The Crisis in Services to the Poor', *American Journal of Orthopsychiatry,* 42 (Oct 1972) pp. 758–9.

17. See the findings by G. L. Appel, *Effects of a Financial Incentive on AFDC Employment: Michigan's Experience between July 1969 and July 1970* (Minneapolis: Institute for Interdisciplinary Studies, 1972), and V. K. Smith, 'Employment and Earnings of AFDC Mothers: First Year Effects of The Earnings Exemption in Two Michigan Counties', Ph.D. Dissertation (East Lansing, Michigan: Michigan State University, 1973), and W. Bell and D. Bushe, *Neglecting the Many, Helping the Few: The Impact of the 1967 Work Incentive* (New York: New York University, Center for Studies in Income Maintenance, 1975).

18. For a good handbook on the question of multiple benefits see Vee Burke

and Alair A. Townsend, 'Public Welfare and Work Incentives: Theory and Practice', in 93rd Congress, Joint Economic Committee, Subcommittee on Fiscal Policy, *Studies in Public Welfare*, Paper No. 14 (Washington: US Government Printing Office, 1974).

19. Joseph H. Ball, 'CETA Planning and Implementation: Pouring New Federalism into Old Battles', unpublished paper (New York: Fordham University, 1975).

20. Except for the General Assistance category in various states, which was not funded by the federal government.

CHAPTER 3

1. Strictly speaking, Great Britain is the United Kingdom without Northern Ireland, and the term will be used in this meaning throughout the work. Northern Ireland has a somewhat separate administration for public assistance (Supplementary Benefits) and for some other programs. In view of the special problems of that unhappy land, it seemed wisest to omit it from consideration here. Great Britain in turn, consists of Scotland, England and Wales, the last two of which are usually (but not always) administratively the same for program purposes. Some local government (local authority) programs differ as between Scotland and England. However, the major programs examined in this work are uniform throughout Great Britain.

2. See, for example, a picture story entitled 'Whose Benefit', in the (London) *Sunday Times Magazine* (Nov 26, 1972).

3. Recipients of social benefits in Britain are called claimants. The term helps to remove the stigma of dependence on benefits by emphasizing the fact that all benefits, whether means-tested or universal, are a matter of right. Persons 'claim' what they are entitled to receive.

4. Beatrice Reubens, *The Hard to Employ: European Programs* (New York: Columbia University Press, 1970) p. 51.

5. This is shown in three forthcoming studies, one for the United States as a whole, one for New York City, and one for Detroit. The first is P. Albin and B. Stein, 'Unemployment and Welfare Benefits' being prepared by the Public Assistance Project of the Institute of Labor Relations at New York University. The second, by C. Peter Rydell *et al.*, *Dynamics of New York City's Caseload*, is to be published by New York City Rand Institute, R–1441–NYC. The third is Daniel H. Saks' 'Relation between the Labor Market and the Welfare System through Time', an unpublished working paper (1974).

6. Citizens of the Irish Republic have had free entry into Great Britain with the right to work and to receive benefits. There is a significant amount of ethnic hostility against the Irish in England.

7. See C. A. Moser, 'Statistics about Immigrants: Objectives, Sources, Methods and Problems', in Central Statistical Office, *Social Trends*, no. 3 (London: HMSO, 1972) pp. 20–30.

8. Constance Sorrentino and Joyanna Moy, 'Unemployment in Nine Industrial Countries', *Monthly Labor Review*, vol. 98, no. 6 (June 1975), pp. 9–18.

9. The distinction was developed by Michael Piore in 'Notes on Welfare Reform and the Design of Income Maintenance Systems', unpublished MS (1972).

10. Central Statistical Office, *Monthly Digest of Statistics*, no. 349, January 1975, p. 146 and *Manpower Report of the President 1974* (Washington: US Government Printing Office, April 1974) p. 315.

11. Central Statistical Office, *Social Trends*, no. 4 (1973) p. 106.
12. For analysis of 'claw-back' and the genesis of Family Income Supplement (FIS) see Martin Rein, 'Work Incentives and Welfare Reform in Britain', B. Stein and S. M. Miller (eds), *Incentives and Planning in Social Policy* (Chicago: Aldine Publishing Co., 1973) pp. 170–3.

CHAPTER 4

1. J. F. Sleeman, *The Welfare State: Its Aims, Benefits and Costs* (London: George Allen & Unwin, 1973) pp. 33–6.
2. *Social Insurance and Allied Services,* Cmnd 6404 (London: HMSO, 1942).
3. Excluding double counting by subtracting from the total of all NI claimants those claimants whose benefits are supplemented by SB. The SB component is relatively small for a high proportion of NI/SB claimants. Data are for 1973.
4. See John Walley, *Social Security: Another British Failure?* (London: Charles Knight & Co., 1972) especially pp. 66–129. Sir John was a senior civil servant who played a key role in the development of the post-war British national insurance system.
5. The purpose of this constraint, like wage stop, is to maintain the incentive to work.
6. Note that the stigma-laden term 'assistance' did not quite disappear.
7. However, complaints are heard that administrative officers occassionally try to pressure claimants into getting work. See Dennis Marsden, *Mothers Alone: Poverty and the Fatherless Family* (London: Allen Lane, The Penguin Press, 1969) pp. 182–6.
8. Computed from the number wage-stopped and the total of unemployed SB claimants in Central Statistical Office, *Social Trends*, no. 5 (London: HMSO, 1974) p. 121.
9. Piore makes the point with respect to public assistance, but it applies to all public income transfer devices. See Michael J. Piore, 'Notes on Welfare Reform and the Design of Income Maintenance Systems', prepared for the Secretary's Committee on Work in America, unpublished xerox copy (Department of Health, Education and Welfare, June 14, 1972) p. 2.
10. Benefits computed at 1974 levels.
11. The rent rebate or allowance would, by then, have risen to the highest rate available to the family with curtailed income, but the rise would not affect the family's net income since SB is calculated net of the rent allowance. Again, we see that the benefit, in this case, is a bookkeeping device.
12. For a view of the ambivalent attitudes of administrators, see Michael J. Hill, 'The Exercise of Discretion in the National Assistance Board' (London: Royal Institute of Public Administration, 1969) pp. 86–7 (reprinted from the Spring 1969 issue of *Public Administration*). A broader discussion of stigma is found in Olive Stevenson, *Claimant or Client* (London: George Allen & Unwin, 1973) pp. 13–37.
13. Payment of the full tax, i.e. flat rate plus graduated contribution entitles a married woman to considerably *lower* benefits than would be available to a man or a single woman.
14. There are three classes of contributions: Class 1 – employees; Class 2 – self-employed; and Class 3 – non-employed persons.
15. The point is stressed by Walley, *Social Security,* pp. 131–4.

16. D. P. Moynihan notes the similarity between FAP and FIS. See his *Politics of a Guaranteed Income* (New York: Random House, 1973) p. 5.
17. 'The British' here pertains to my conversations with leading British academics, social workers, and civil servants who were concerned with the enactment and administration of FIS.
18. For an excellent summary of this argument, see Martin Rein, 'Work Incentives and Welfare Reform', in B. Stein and S. M. Miller, *Incentives and Planning in Social Policy* (Chicago: Aldine, 1973) pp. 170–3.
19. House of Commons, *Hansard* (Feb 10, 1975) p. 44.
20. Bruno Stein, 'Tax Credits: Poverty Trap', *Spectator* (Sep 8, 1973) pp. 322–3.
21. See 'For Your Client's Benefit', *Social Work*, 1 (Apr 5, 1973) p. 7.
22. Computed from unpublished data compiled by the Department of Health and Social Security (1973), and *Hansard*, op. cit., p. 46.
23. This is a rough estimate made for September 1971 and is said to represent the single best available figure from a wide range of possibilities. See John Stacpoole, 'Running FIS', *New Society* (Jan 13, 1972), p. 65.
24. Department of Health & Social Security, *Supplementary Benefits Handbook*, rev. ed., Supplementary Benefits Commission, SBA Paper No. 2 (London: HMSO, 1972) pp. 12–14.
25. At the time of the study, fifteen was school-leaving age in Britain.
26. A number of the persons I interviewed in the Department of Employment believed that Training Allowances were 'greater' than SB in order to provide an incentive to train. This indicates a policy perception contrary to facts, a condition that is as common in the United States as it is in Britain. Strictly speaking, training allowances can be supplemented by SB, but the practice appears to be relatively rare.
27. Approximately 80 per cent of applicants for Government Training Centres in 1971 were below age forty. Unpublished data from the Queen Mary College Survey of Government Training Centres, courtesy of Mr Adrian Ziderman.
28. Except to the extent that they are modified by wage stop which would reduce the level of SB for unskilled labor.
29. Queen Mary College Survey.
30. The QMC Survey shows that the ratio of unemployed to employed applicants at Government Training Centres was 2:1 in the North and Northwest regions, and 1:1 in London. Ibid.
31. Henry Aaron, *Why Is Welfare So Hard to Reform* (Washington: Brookings Institution, 1973) pp. 31–5.
32. US Congress, Joint Economic Committee, Studies in Public Welfare No. 14, *Public Welfare and Work Incentives: Theory and Practice* (Washington, US Government Printing Office, 1974).
33. London: Institute for Economic Affairs, 1970.
34. D. Piachaud, 'Poverty and Taxation', *Political Quarterly* 41 (Jan 1971) pp. 31–44. Also see his 'Tax Credits and Disincentives', *Conference on Proposals for a Tax-Credit System* (London: Institute for Fiscal Studies, 1973) pp. 64–72. The original Piachaud work was further developed by J. Bradshaw and I. Wakeman in 'The Poverty Trap Updated', *Political Quarterly* 43, (Dec 1972) pp. 459–69. Perhaps the best available estimates of the relevant rates are in G. C. Fiegehen and P. S. Lansley, 'The Tax Credit Proposals', *National Institute Economic Review*, 64 (May 1973) pp. 66–7.

35. *Proposals for a Tax-Credit System* Cmnd 5116 (London: HMSO Oct 1972) pp. 2, 24–5.
36. The proposals would not have eliminated the problem. See Fiegehen and Lansley, op. cit., pp. 59–60, and Peter Meyers, 'The Economics of Tax Credits', unpublished paper (1973).
37. The New Jersey Income Maintenance Experiment in the United States concluded that the income guarantee with a negative tax provision had an insignificant effect on the labor force participation of husbands and a small effect on that of wives in the experimental group. No clear conclusion could be drawn, however, with respect to differing marginal tax rates. See US Department of Health, Education and Welfare, *Summary Report: New Jersey Graduated Work Incentive Experiment* (Washington: US Government Printing Office, 1973).
38. These are housing subsidies made available to low-income families by local authorities. Rates are local property taxes.
39. See the works cited in note 34 above.
40. National Board for Prices and Incomes, *General Problems of Low Pay,* Cmnd 4648 (London: HMSO Apr 1971), Tables 6(2) and 6(5).
41. A theoretical discussion of this phenomenon is found in a forthcoming paper by N. A. Barr and B. Stein, entitled 'Income Support and the Poverty Trap'. Also see B. Stein, 'Tax Credits', op. cit., and Central Statistical Office, *Social Trends,* No. 5 (London: HMSO, 1974), pp. 119, 122.
42. Raymond Munts, 'Partial Benefits in Unemployment Insurance', *Journal of Human Resources,* 4 (Spring 1970) pp. 160–76.

CHAPTER 5
1. Unpublished data, Department of Health and Social Security.
2. Unpublished data, Department of Health and Social Security. Also see *Report of the Committee on Abuse of Social Security Benefits* (Fisher Committee) Cmnd 5228 (London; HMSO Mar 1973) pp. 120–1.
3. Department of Health and Social Security, *Training of Staff*, Supplementary Benefits Administration Papers No. 3 (London: HMSO, 1973) pp. 34–5.
4. Olive Stevenson, *Claimant or Client? A Social Worker's View of the Supplementary Benefit Commission* (London: George Allen and Unwin, 1973), pp. 115, 230–2.
5. *Supplementary Benefits Handbook*, p. 55.
6. According to the Department of Health and Social Security *Annual Report* for 1971, 2066 men attended. See p. 123. The Fisher Committee Report gives the number as 2126 voluntary, plus 47 'under direction'. See *Report . . . on Abuse of Social Security Benefits*, pp. 116–17.
7. Ibid., p. 207.
8. Department of Health and Social Security, unpublished statistics.
9. Stevenson, *Claimant or Client?*, pp. 123–4.
10. Computed from data in Central Statistical Office, *Social Trends*, no. 5, (London: HMSO, 1974) p. 121.
11. *Supplementary Benefits Handbook*, pp. 25–6. Also see Ministry of Social Security, *Adminstration of the Wage Stop*, Supplementary Benefits Administration Paper No. 1 (London: HMSO, 1967; reprinted 1972).
12. Supplementary Benefits Paper No. 1, p. 2.
13. See Walley, *Social Security*, p. 119.
14. *Supplementary Benefits Handbook*, pp. 25–6.

CHAPTER 6

1. For an excellent discussion of British manpower policy, see Organization for Economic Cooperation and Development, *Manpower Policy in the United Kingdom*, Reviews of Manpower and Social Policies No. 7 (Paris: OECD Publications, 1970). Also see the references to Britain in Margaret S. Gordon, *Retraining and Labor Market Adjustments in Western Europe*, US Department of Labor, Manpower and Automation Research Monograph No. 4 (Washington: US Government Printing Office, 1965).

2. Gary B. Hansen, *Britian's Industrial Training Act: Its History, Development and Implication for America* (Washington: National Manpower Policy Task Force, 1967) pp. 60–2, 64–5.

3. Santosh Mukerjee, *Changing Manpower Needs: A Study of Industrial Training Boards* (London: PEP, 1970) pp. 110–11.

4. For a critical view of the Redundancy Payments Act, see Santosh Mukerjee, *Through No Fault of their Own: Systems for Handling Redundancies in Britain, France and Germany* (London: MacDonald & Co., 1973).

5. Department of Employment, *Training for the Future: A Plan for Discussion* (London: HMSO, 1972) p. 18.

6. 'News and Notes', *Department of Employment Gazette* (Jun 1973).

7. This is the new name for the Vocational Training Scheme under which the GTCs were operated.

8. OECD, *Manpower Policy*, p. 76.

9. Audrey Hunt, Judith Fox and Michael Bradley, *Post-Training Careers of Government Training Centre Trainees*, Office of Popoulation Censuses and Surveys, Social Security Division (London: HMSO, 1972), p. 17. The report states that 76·7 per cent of trainees had been in a job immediately before entry, 5·3 per cent came straight from the armed forces. 10·5 per cent were unemployed, and the remaining 7·5 per cent had been sick or came from an Industrial Rehabilitation Unit. IRUs will be described below.

10. Ibid., p. 19.

11. M. J. Hill, R. M. Harrison, A. J. Sargeant, and V. Talbot, *Men Out of Work: A Study of Unemployment in Three English Towns* (Cambridge: Cambridge University Press, 1973).

12. Ibid., pp. 99–101. Unpublished data courtesy of Michael Hill. Persons who were accepted by GTCs and had begun training would not have been picked up by the sample.

13. Department of Employment, Feb 1, 1972. Strictly speaking, TOPS was announced in August 1972. The consultative paper 'Training for the Future' uses the older term 'Vocational Training Scheme'.

14. The obverse is also done: employers can arrange for GTC courses for their own employees.

15. *Employment and Training Act, 1973 (Chapter 50)* (London: HMSO, 1973).

16. Strictly speaking, there is no geographic catchment area, and trainees may go to any GTC that has room and offers training in the desired trade. A special allowance for lodging is granted to persons who train away from home. However, the majority of trainees attend Centres within commuting distance of their homes.

17. OECD, *Manpower Policy*, p. 179.

18. See House of Commons, *Seventh Report from the Expenditure Committee,* (London: HMSO, 1973) pp. xxvii–xxix, 251–3.

19. See Beatrice G. Rubens, *The Hard to Employ: European Programs* (New York: Columbia University Press, 1970) especially the discussion of definitions on pp. 1–6.
20. House of Commons, *Seventh Report*, p. 56.
21. Ibid., pp. lv–lvi.
22. *Post-Training Careers*, p. 142.
23. Department of Employment, *Resettlement Policy and Services for Disabled* (n.p.: Jul 20, 1972) p. 111.
24. Ibid., p. 115.
25. Department of Employment, 'Outline of a Pilot Study Conducted by the Department of Employment at Washwood Heath Employment Exchange', HOW–140–30 2/72 ED, Xerox of typescript (Feb 1972).
26. Ibid.
27. Department of Employment, *Resettlement Policy*, p. 122.
28. The term refers here to occupational guidance and placement.
29. Ibid.
30. A fourteenth opened in 1973, and three more are in planning.
31. Section 34, *Social Security Act of 1966*.
32. House of Commons, *Seventh Report*, pp. lxxiv–lxxvii.
33. I estimate the average stay is ten weeks. This is arrived at by dividing the number of training places by the number of trainees.
34. Ibid., p. lxxv.
35. Ibid., pp. 193–4.

CHAPTER 7

1. A number of other states had policies which, while less punitive, also had the effect of levying a marginal tax on earnings of less than 100 per cent.
2. See Leonard J. Hausman, 'Cumulative Tax Rates in Alternative Income Maintenance Systems', in US Congress, Joint Economic Committee, Studies in Public Welfare No. 4, *Income Transfer Programs: How They Tax the Poor* (Washington: US Government Printing Office, 1974) pp. 91–136.
3. British control mechanisms are probably less cruel, on the whole, than American ones.
4. US Congress, Joint Economic Committee, Studies in Public Welfare No. 3, *The Effectiveness of Manpower Training Programs* (Washington: US Government Printing Office, 1972) pp. 2–15 (esp. p. 3), 34.
5. Ibid., pp. 4–6.
6. Ibid., pp. 8–11 and the author's own observations. It should be stressed that some firms did attempt the training in good faith.
7. They may, of course, have other uses. In the United States, some of the programs are clearly disguised forms of income maintenance. In some instances, they are also a form of political patronage to political organizations with low-income constituencies.
8. *Manpower Report of the President, 1974* (Washington: US Government Printing Office, 1974), pp. 133–4.
9. Ibid., p. 132.
10. The WIN program helps to remove male heads of households from the welfare rolls by disqualifying them from welfare if they work more than 100 hours per month. Female heads, on the other hand, retain part of their earnings so that their combined work and welfare income can be substantially greater than income from either work or welfare. The subsidy to employers presumably gives welfare mothers a competitive edge over non-welfare recipients in the labor market.

Index

Boskin